May 5, 1988

To My Sister,
Yong Ae Kwon,
Aiming for
Success
and Succeeding
is my only
wish for you.
You Deserve all that
there is in the
world.
Take Great
care, Sis.
I Love You,
Nami.

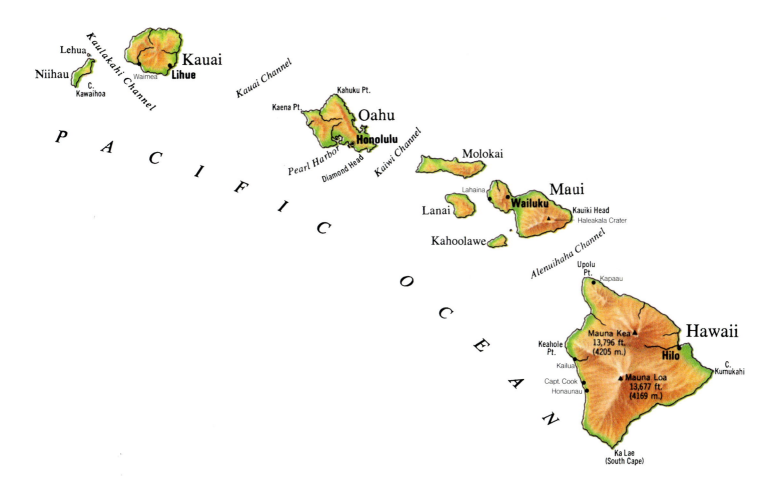

Lehua

Niihau

C.
Kawaihoa

Kaulakahi Channel

Waimea

Kauai

Lihue

Kauai Channel

Kahuku Pt.

Kaena Pt.

Oahu

Honolulu

Pearl Harbor

Diamond Head

Kaiwi Channel

Molokai

Lahaina

Lanai

Maui

Wailuku

Kauiki Head

Haleakala Crater

Kahoolawe

Alenuihaha Channel

Upolu
Pt.

Kapaau

Keahole
Pt.

Mauna Kea ▲
13,796 ft.
(4205 m.)

Hawaii

Kailua

▲ Mauna Loa
13,677 ft.
(4169 m.)

Hilo

C.
Kumukahi

Capt. Cook

Honaunau

Ka Lae
(South Cape)

P   A   C   I   F   I   C   O   C   E   A   N

Hawaii Aloha

Photography
Greg Vaughn
Paul Chesley, Robert Shallenberger, Brett Uprichard
and many others

Essays and Tales
Dan Boylan, Carolyn Corn, Carol Hogan,
Edward Joesting, Bob Krauss, Will Kyselka,
Andrew Lind, Donald Mitchell,
Brian Nicol, Alan Ziegler

Press Pacifica
Pearl City, Hawaii

Produced by Jürgen F. Boden and Elke Emshoff
Designed by Hartmut Brückner

Published in the United States of America, 1987
by Press Pacifica, P.O. Box 668,
Pearl City, Hawaii 96782
(Exclusive distributors in the state of Hawaii)

Library of Congress Cataloging-in-Publication Data

Hawaii aloha.

Bibliography: p.
1. Hawaii – Description and travel – 1987 – Views.
2. Hawaii – Description and travel – 1987. – I. Vaughn,
Greg. II. Boylan, Dan.
DU623.25.H37 1987 996.9 87-2910

ISBN 0-916630-54-4

© 1987 by Alouette Verlag

Map of Hawaii by permission of Hammond, Inc.
Ink drawing AHI on front/end papers courtesy of Dietrich Varez

Published simultaneously in the United States of America by Press Pacifica, Pearl City, Hawaii, and in the Federal Republic of Germany, Switzerland and Austria by Alouette Verlag, Oststeinbek/Hamburg, West Germany.
Printed in the Federal Republic of Germany.

Acknowledgments

Hawaii is the Aloha State; aloha is a special word that can say hello or goodbye or love. But it means much more: warmth and caring, music and dance, flowers and birds, a fascinating history and a unique culture. Our goal in this book was to show all of this and more. We assembled some of Hawaii's most talented photographers and writers and encouraged them to share their expertise and knowledge with our international audience. The result, we feel, is a comprehensive portrait of Hawaii, its people and their aloha.

Besides thanking both the photographers and writers for their cooperation, we are most grateful to Brian Nicol, who acted not only as our text editor but also as coordinator for the many aspects in the making of this book. We are also obliged to the Hawaii Visitors Bureau and to various departments of the State of Hawaii for facilitating our extensive »field work« in the Islands. Our thanks go as well to Linda Perreira, Tom Coffman, Leonard Lueras and Dr. Charles Lamoureux for their assistance in special aspects of the project.

Jürgen F. Boden and Elke Emshoff

Contents

Hawaii Facts Sheet

The Hawaiian chain stretches 1,523 miles southeast to northwest from Cape Kumukahi on the island of Hawaii to Kure atoll and consists of eight major islands and 124 minor islands. Seven of the eight (except for Kahoolawe) are the inhabited portions of the state.

Island (nickname)	Area (square miles)	Population (July 1,1985 estimates)
Hawaii (Big Island)	4,035	109,200
Maui (Valley Isle)	735	76,600
Oahu (Gathering Place)	618	814,600
Kauai (Garden Isle)	558	44,600
Molokai (Friendly Isle)	264	6,500
Lanai (Pineapple Island)	141	2,200
Niihau	71	180
Kahoolawe	46	–
Northwestern Hawaiian Islands	3	24
Total	6,471	1,053,904

Capital city	Honolulu
Highest official temperature at Honolulu International Airport	94°F
Lowest official temperature at Honolulu International Airport	53°F

Average annual rainfall:
Wettest spot – Mount Waialeale, Kauai	444″
Driest spot – Puako, Hawaii	9.5″

Largest volcanic eruptions (1859 and 1950), in million cubic yards of lava	each	600
Worst earthquake (1868), Richter scale		7.5
Highest tsunami wave (1946), feet		56
Most destructive hurricane (Iwa, 1982) in miles per hour		117

Hawaii's motto on the State Seal:
Ua mau ke ea o ka aina i ka pono
(»The life of the land is perpetuated in righteousness«)

HAWAII, A LOVE AFFAIR by Brian Nicol

For me, it began as a reprieve from war. In 1970 my wife and I shared a six-day R & R on these islands. When it was over, I returned to Vietnam to finish out my one-year tour of duty; she returned to our home in Minneapolis to work and wait. During those six special days we discovered Island beauty and met Island people. The beauty amazed us and the people impressed us. The greens and blues of the land and the sea were incredibly rich, like nothing we'd seen before. The people – shopkeepers, waitresses, tour guides – were constantly saying, »Have a nice day,« and meaning it. The aloha spirit seemed embodied in every Islander we met.

Then when we went our separate ways at Honolulu International Airport, we vowed to return to the Islands. After all, we reasoned, people do in fact live here, every day, all their lives, making money, raising families. We would join them some day.

That day came in August 1974. We quit our Minnesota jobs (teacher, waitress), packed four suitcases and caught a Western Airlines flight bound for Honolulu. We had $ 1,000. If we managed to land Island jobs, we'd stay. If not, we'd enjoy the money for a few weeks, re-pack our bags and catch a plane headed in the other direction. But we got jobs – and we've been here ever since.

Hawaii is easy to fall in love with. More than 5 million tourists do so every year. Yet for that love to last, to grow beyond infatuation and endure, there have to be sweet memories – magic moments sprinkled throughout the years of daily Island living. For me, those moments are many, but here are a few:

☐ Eight of us are sitting on a spacious wooden lanai high up a Molokai slope. We are watching the sun set behind Oahu, 30 miles away on the horizon. We have developed a system of rating Hawaii sunsets, a simple 1 to 10 scale. A 5 is a good one, a 6 or 7 is excellent, a 10 will happen only at the second coming of Christ. As we watch the sun disappear and the colors begin on this March evening in 1976, we realize we are witnessing greatness. The sky shimmers in rich oranges, reds and pinks. Puffy white cumulus clouds all in straight rows are flashing like semaphores. We are well past 6 and on to 7 or 8 on our scale. The high, stringy cirrus clouds seem to be streaking through the sky. The glow surrounds us – above and on all sides. Someone whispers »8«; no one argues. We are obliged to be silent, as if we have entered a cathedral. The colors continue to vibrate in the sky and reflect off our faces: 9. »I think I hear angels singing,« says someone softly. The spectacle lasts for half an hour. We sit, staring numbly, realizing darkness must surely come but half-expecting to see Jesus, descending slowly from above.

☐ My wife and I are having dinner with a Samoan friend and his family in their project townhouse in Kalihi, a low-income, working class neighborhood noted for its rough ways and easy charm. Our friend is small for a Samoan: about six feet tall and 220 lbs. But he is tough and proud: He's a black belt karate expert and likes to tell tales about various street fights and bar brawls. But there is no violence tonight, of course. His wife and their four kids and his father-in-law treat us like royalty. They do not have many haole (Causasian) visitors and they are curious and a bit nervous. Only our friend speaks passable English, and we know no Samoan. But the children communicate with their laughter and smiles. There are enough steaks, chicken breasts and boiled bananas to feed an army. The food and drink eases the nervousness and soon we are all talking and laughing in a Samoan-English language we make up as we go along. By evening's end, our friend's father-in-law has spread out a map of Western Samoa on the table and is showing us the locations of his family plots of land. Someday he'll return to that land, he insists. We believe him. He makes us promise to visit him there someday. He writes down Samoan addresses and names and makes marks on the map. He tells us about the sights we'll see. He speaks no English, but he describes them beautifully.

That was many years ago and we still haven't been to Samoa. But we may someday; after all, we have an invitation.

☐ My friend Bob and I are dressed only in shorts and slippers. Along with about 4,000 other lightly clad people we are sweating in the hot sun in the middle of Diamond Head Crater. It's 1977 and we are attending what will be the last Crater Festival; neighborhood complaints will put an end to these annual concerts inside Hawaii's most famous landmark.

As we make our way through the crowd, rock music pulsates from the stage far down in front. Beer cans and beach mats are underfoot; marijuana smoke and dust swirl around us. Suddenly two beautiful Island females pass in front of us, wearing skimpy bikinis – the bottoms only. We're both quiet for a few seconds, then Bob sighs and says, »Lucky we live in Hawaii.«

☐ It's mid-January 1982 and my wife and I and our three-week-old little boy are on the Big Island. I'm doing legwork for a magazine article and have brought the two of them along. We have been in and out of our rental car all day long as I interview people and check out sites. But now it's late afternoon and we have returned to the Hotel Honokaa Club, a small building in the small town of Honokaa on the Big Island's northeast side. We decide to have a cold beer in the hotel's tiny bar before going up to our room. We are a bit apprehensive as we sit down at a table; an hour earlier a bartender at another Honokaa tavern wouldn't serve us because our three-week old infant was not 18 years of age or older. »It's the law,« he said. »Goodbye,« I said.

So now we are relieved when the waitress at the Hotel Honokaa Club bar quickly brings us two cold ones and is immediately enamored of our smiling little boy. She insists we prop his infant carrier up on the table so the regulars seated at the bar – three older Hawaiian men – can see him. They begin asking us about our boy and our Big Island trip. Soon we feel like regulars, part of the club family. They buy us beers.

»What's the baby's name?« one of them asks.

»Kevin Thomas,« my wife answers.

»He was born in Hawaii?« he asks.

»Yes, at Kapiolani Children's Hospital in Honolulu,« I answer.

»Well, if he was born in Hawaii, you should give him a Hawaii name too,« he says.

I start to answer something about thinking it wouldn't be proper because we're haoles, and he interrupts me politely but firmly: »Bless him with a Hawaiian name.« We did; he's Kevin Thomas Pakelika Nicol now. Pakelika is Hawaiian for Patrick. Patrick, one of Kevin's many uncles, lived with us here for three years and shared many of our best Island days.

Living in Hawaii isn't all fond memories and sweetness and light, of course. We in Hawaii pay high taxes and earn low wages. Our cost of living is one of the highest in the nation. Every morning and every evening on Oahu too many cars fight for too little space on too few roads. Many of our scenic lookouts are littered with beer cans and fast-food wrappers, primarily the leavings of Hawaii people, not tourists. In Hawaii, we sometimes become tangled in government red tape, waiting in long lines to fill out more forms and be assessed more fees. Our ethnic melting pot is seasoned lightly but noticeably with racism. We constantly fight rock fever, feeling trapped on a rock in the middle of an ocean, an airline ticket our only escape.

Yet despite all that, Hawaii is a paradise. And I'm reminded of that simple truth every morning as I step out of my front door and look at my small slice of ocean view, between the mango trees and the highrises. The early sun is sparkling on the sea, the first sailboats are leaving their slips and a few planes are gliding across the sky. The air is warm and fresh. I'm on my way to work – in Hawaii. And I'm smiling.

———————

In the essays that follow, you'll read the words of others who are in the midst of Hawaii love affairs. You'll learn about history and culture, flowers and birds, politics and sports. You'll meet intriguing people and witness fascinating events. You'll get the facts and the stats. But between the lines in each and every one of these essays, and in the background of every spectacular photo, are two special words: memories and magic.

Polynesian introduced coconut palm and native *'ohia* forest along the Hana Coast Road on Maui. The nectar of the *'ohia-lehua* (blossoms) serves as a vital year-round food source for forest birds and insects. Within Akaka Falls State Park, north of Hilo on the Big Island, a trail winds through a tropical forest of guava, ginger and bamboo on its way to the 412-foot high Akaka Falls.

Grosvenor Center's twin mirror-glassed towers and the old Dillingham Transportation Building at their base are located in downtown Honolulu.

Magnificent Waikiki beach, a two-mile strip of coastline, is actually a series of six smaller beaches stretching all the way to Diamond Head. It was once favored by Hawaiian royalty for its fine fishing and gentle, rideable waves. Once swampy marshlands and taro fields, Waikiki today offers more than 35,000 hotel and condominium units for visitors from around the world.

Beach life at Wailea, located just past Kihei on Maui's southwestern shore. Wailea is a self-contained resort with hotels, condominiums, restaurants, shopping and five beaches.

Surf shop in Waikiki.

Though often crowded, Waikiki still fulfills the dreams of the sun-hungry visitors as well as residents and lives up to its nickname as »life's greatest beach.«

Tandem surfing at
Makaha beach on
Oahu's Waianae Coast,
one of the Islands'
most famous surf
breaks.

Windsurfer Stuart
Sawyer, now back in
England, belongs to the
world elite in wave
riding and jumping.

The Na Pali coast on Kauai, a 14-mile stretch of almost inaccessible terrain, is the result of nature's chiseling through the forces of erosion, leaving sharp pleats of land with lush vegetation. Between the cliffs that jut out into the surf are beaches, pristine and isolated from all but the most determined adventurers.

At Mo'okini *heiau* (temple) on the northern tip of the Big Island *ali'i nui* (kings and ruling chiefs) fasted, prayed and offered human sacrifices to their gods. The temple was constructed under the direction of high priest Kuamo'o Mo'okini and was dedicated to Ku, the god of war.

The well-known statue of Kamehameha the Great in Honolulu is actually a replica; the original (shown here) was commissioned by King Kalakaua, sculpted by Thomas B. Gould of Florence and cast in Paris in 1880. While being transported from Bremen it was lost in a storm near the Falkland Islands, later recovered and finally erected at Kapaau near Kamehameha's birthplace on the Big Island. A further replica of the king stands in Statuary Hall in the nation's Capitol, Washington, D.C.

These native ferns grow in the Upper Forest Reserve at an altitude of 8,500 feet on the northeastern slope of Haleakala on Maui. This forest area has been intensively studied in the past 15 years and is the habitat in which the *po'ouli*, an enigmatic brownish, black-faced new species of Hawaiian honeycreeper, was discovered in 1973.

Two of the more colorful surviving species of Hawaiian honeycreeper are the *'i'iwi*, seen here feeding on the nectar of the native *mamane* tree's yellow blossoms, and the *'apapane*. Both can frequently be found in the upland areas of Kauai, Maui and the Big Island. The plumage of these and several other forest birds was once used in the famed cloaks and other featherwork of Hawaiian royalty.

This Gulf Fritillary butterfly is a recent accidental introduction and is not as colorful as the native Kamehameha butterfly.

The Big Island of Hawaii lies over one of the earth's great »hotspots,« and here on this island the legendary goddess of volcanoes, Pele, makes her home.

Among the five volcanoes, Mauna Kea (at 13,796 feet the highest mountain of Hawaii) and Kohala mountains have been extinct for thousands of years, while Hualalai

last erupted in 1801. Fiery eruptions can frequently be observed at Kilauea, and on March 30, 1984, both Kilauea and Mauna Loa (13,677 feet) spit molten lava at the same

time, something that had not happened in 114 years. Both volcanoes are now protected in the Hawaii Volcanoes National Park.

The native fern is often the first plant to grow on barren lava fields. Given the proper climate, the 'ohia may germinate before ferns, mosses and lichens.

THE ISLANDS OF HAWAII: BORN OF FIRE by Will Kyselka

A chain of islands stretches 1,600 miles across the middle of the Pacific Ocean like a gigantic slashmark. Kure Atoll stands at one end of this Hawaiian chain; the island of Hawaii at the other.

Kure is the oldest, Hawaii the youngest, with age decreasing in the southeasterly direction. The older islands are the small, highly eroded remnants of volcanic peaks that once rose high above the sea. Many have been eroded into jagged pinnacles that jut out of the ocean, and others have been reduced to reefs and shoals. A continual battle between construction and destruction takes place along the Hawaiian chain and once volcanic activity ceases, an island is doomed to being reclaimed by the sea.

The younger islands are those at the southeastern end of the chain – Kauai, Niihau, Oahu, Molokai, Lanai, Maui, Kahoolawe and Hawaii. Not only are these islands young, they're also high, with the tallest peaks rising nearly 14,000 feet above sea level. Rainfall is abundant, vegetation is lush and a little more than a million human beings inhabit seven of these eight islands. The older islands beyond Kauai, in contrast, are dry and inhabited by birds, monk seals and turtles. In its natural state, Hawaii is one of the most isolated places on this planet. There is no land to the east for 2,500 miles. Land in the opposite direction lies almost twice that distance away, except for tiny Wake Island and a cluster of coral atolls at the north end of the Marianas.

The islands of Hawaii are the eroded summits of gigantic dome-shaped volcanoes that rise from bases on the ocean floor more than 3 miles beneath the surface. They resemble the shields carried by ancient Germanic warriors, and they're known as »shield volcanoes.« Shields are built of countless flows of highly fluid basaltic lava that erupts at high temperature, runs swiftly from a vent and then spreads out rapidly.

All the islands in the Hawaiian chain first formed in the place where the island of Hawaii is today. Lava, extruded onto the floor of the ocean, builds the shield. But the volcano doesn't stay where it was built – the floor of the Pacific is riding on one of the great crustal plates of the earth and is moving northwest at a rate comparable to the rate of growth of a person in one lifetime. The islands are born onto this Pacific plate and carried on a natural conveyor belt, eventually to disappear beneath continents.

North of Kure, the shields are so old they're no longer islands. Planed off by the sea, they've sunk as much as 3,000 feet beneath the waves, their truncated tops forming a line of »seamounts« – the Emperor Seamounts. Why the disappearing islands? Partly erosion, but mostly because of the plastic flow of the earth's mantle just beneath its crust. The tremendous weight of the shield bends the crust, and the slow movement of the mantle accommodates to the load in much the same way that ice on the surface of a skating pond bends to accommodate the weight of the skater.

Rainwater gullies an island and the sea batters its edges. Chemical and biological processes hasten weathering in such a moist, warm climate.

Hawaii lies in the belt of the northeast trade winds. The trades are low surface winds that blow over thousands of miles of »fetch« area and gather the moisture that keeps Hawaii cool.

Trade winds originate in a high-pressure region 30 degrees on either side of the equator. Deflected to the west by the spinning earth, the northern hemisphere wind blows from the northeast. Its mirror image in the southern hemisphere is the southeast trade wind system.

Warm and moist as it reaches the Hawaiian chain, the air passes over low islands as if they weren't even there. But the high islands constitute a barrier to that free flow. The air pushes against the mountains, rises and condenses into clouds. A good example of this effect is the 3,000-foot Koolau mountain range on the island of Oahu. Generally such a cloud-cover hides the crest of the range. Because the trade winds are low, several peaks at the southern end of the chain are so high that trade wind clouds can only form a ring around their mid-slopes.

The presence of mountains profoundly affects the rainfall pattern in Hawaii. The average rainfall in the open ocean around the islands is 35 inches a year. But because of cloud-scraping mountains the rainfall gradient is steep, and you can go from rain forest to desert in a matter of a few miles. The steepest gradient is on the island of Maui, with the summit of West Maui Mountain receiving up to 600 inches a year and with Olowalu, only 6 miles distant, receiving 2 inches.

Hawaii lies within the tropics, between the »turning places of the sun.« The sun shines straight down on Hawaii from May through July and heats the mass of water that is the Pacific Ocean. Water is a great absorber of heat. It stores the sun's energy and releases it slowly so that the average winter temperature is 73 °F, and 81 °F in the summer. Occasionally the temperature sinks into the 60s F in Honolulu. That's a cold spell and it becomes an item of news in the daily newspapers. The surface temperature of the ocean at Waikiki varies from 70 to 85 degrees Fahrenheit during the year.

During the winter months when temperate regions are blanketed in snow, the trade winds are pushed southward and sometimes blocked. That's the time of *kona* winds, when tropical storms sometimes deluge the islands with rain. Diamond Head, on the south shore of Oahu, »greens up« at such times but the rest of the year is a desert region immersed in a warm, humid, tropical wind system.

Torrential rains may dump an inch of rainfall per hour on the islands. Many rain gauges have recorded 20 inches in a 24-hour period. Occasional tropical storms may drop as much as 24 inches of rain in 4 hours, a rare event. The heaviest ever recorded was at Kilauea on the island of Kauai: 40 inches fell in a 24-hour period, with 6 of those inches falling within a single half hour. Each island has been created in a unique pattern of eruptions, and each is uniquely shaped by erosion.

THE ISLAND OF HAWAII

The island of Hawaii lies over one of the great »hotspots« on earth. Here heat escapes from the interior of the earth, molten rock rises from great depths and pauses in magma chambers (sources of lava), then fountains from vents to build volcanic shields. Here all the islands in the chain were born – born in fire onto the ocean floor and carried on a huge tectonic plate to where they are today. Here volcanic activity is directly observable. And here on the Big Island of Hawaii the legendary goddess of volcanoes, Pele, makes her home.

The Big Island is well named. Not only is it large in extent but its volcanoes are of tremendous volume. Twice as large as all the other islands combined, the Big Island includes the world's tallest mountain, Mauna Kea, and the most voluminous geologic structure on earth, Mauna Loa.

The five volcanoes on Hawaii are geologically young, all having appeared within the last million years. Three of them – Hualalai, Kilauea and Mauna Loa – have been active in historic time. Kilauea is the most consistently active over the past two centuries, and within the past two years has completed 25 eruptive phases. Best of all, though, this most active volcano is also the most accessible.

Kilauea

Drive 30 miles south from the town of Hilo on Hawaii's east coast, and in an hour's time you're at the summit of Kilauea, 4,000 feet above sea level. Kilauea is built on the side of Mauna Loa. The two volcanoes are in close proximity but their activity is not at all related. Apparently their plumbing is separate and they tap different magma reservoirs.

A great summit depression lies at the top of Kilauea. Oval in shape and 3 miles in diameter, the floor of this crater is flat and bounded by nearly vertical walls 500 feet high. Kilauea's sunken-in summit is a caldera, typical of shield volcanoes. Such a caldera forms as magma beneath the summit moves on, leaving a void into which the unsupported summit sinks.

Perched on the edge of Kilauea's caldera is the Hawaiian Volcano Observatory. Sensitive instruments at the observatory keep a constant check on Kilauea's activity, as well as on that of Mauna Loa and even of Loihi, an active volcano still 3,000 feet beneath the surface of the sea. The Kilauea caldera is vast and serene, yet awesome potential boils beneath the black lava flows that floor the crater and from which the steam emerges.

The Halemaumau Fire Pit lies at the far end of the caldera. For a century it contained a lava lake that beautifully displayed convective overturn, spectacular at night. Lava, rising to the surface of the lake, would quickly cool to blackness upon contact with the air, then form a crust. Convective forces would move these newly formed crustal plates to the edges of the lake where they would rise on edge, revealing the incandescent glow of 1,100°C lava and slide downward into the lake, once more to be reincorporated into lava. Halemaumau Fire Pit steams and fumes today, depositing sulphur along its sides. Occasionally the lake reappears for a short while, rising and falling according to its mood.

For an unusually intimate experience with a volcano, hike the 3-mile trail down the escarpment by the Volcano House and out onto the caldera floor. Here you're walking in clouds of steam, the intensity of which varies with the temperature of the air and its humidity. Steam is produced as ground water sinks into cracks, is vaporized in contact with the hot rock, then returns to the air to condense in clouds. A cold rain may sweep in and you may lose the trail for a moment in the clouds, but the cairns that stand as black beacons will guide you along the edges of the black, crunchy trail. Steam vents are warm and comforting when the weather is cold, but the instant you leave that comfort the added dampness of condensation makes you even colder than before.

Hike across the caldera by yourself to know what it feels like to be walking on the crust of a live volcano located over one of the great hotspots on earth. A vast desolation of new lava, the boundary cliffs of the caldera in the distance, the quietness, the lack of vegetation, the acrid smell of sulphur products – they are all there for you to discover. And as you saunter through the caldera you wonder, »Is it going to erupt *now*?«

You'll find it fascinating to walk over black lava rock, still hot not far beneath the surface, then to cross fresh, barren lava fields of *pahoehoe* and *a'a* - onomatopoetic Hawaiian words that are used worldwide to describe the billowy, entwined form of pahoehoe and the jumbled, sharp-edged, painfully jagged form of a'a. Separated from Kilauea by narrow Byron's Ledge is the small crater, Kilauea Iki. Hike the trail from the Volcano House down the fault scarps of the caldera through forests of tree fern and *'ohia*, across Byron's Ledge and out onto the floor of Kilauea Iki. An eruption in 1959 on the side of this pit crater flooded the floor with lava and formed a lake. When the lava lake rose to the height of the vent, it choked off the eruption and the lava drained back down the vent, only to reappear in a matter of hours in a new eruptive phase. Blobs and clots of lava hurled out of the Kilauea Iki eruption rose to heights of 1,900 feet, spinning into volcanic bombs with curlicue ends. Separating in mid-air, clumps of lava would string out long black threads of basaltic rock known as Pele's Hair. Ash carried to the leeward side of the vent built an asymmetric cone and devastated a forest of 'ohia trees. For a closer look at the products of that cinder cone - ash, dust, cinders - hike the boardwalk »Devastation Trail.«

A short distance from Kilauea Iki is Thurston Lava Tube, 30 feet in diameter. A lava tube forms as the surface of a lava flow freezes over, forming a crust. Beneath that insulating crust, hot lava continues flowing. When the eruption ceases the molten rock drains away, leaving a tube that may be as much as 30 feet in diameter in some places, as little as a foot or two in others. In some old lava tubes entymologists have found sightless insects and spiders that have adapted to the perpetual darkness.

Mauna Loa

An ever-present reminder of the immensity of a shield volcano is Mauna Loa, the »long mountain« to the west, a prolific lava producer. A long, smooth slope runs toward the south, and the mountain itself resembles an inverted canoe. It is hard to comprehend the magnitude of this mountain. There is no sense of towering height here as with the spectacular up-swept cones of Mount Fuji and Mount Rainier and Mount Mayon. The shield is massive, not towering, and what appears to be a big rounded hill in the distance hides the fact that its summit is at an altitude of 13,677 feet, almost 2 miles higher than Kilauea.

There are 10,000 cubic miles of rock within Mauna Loa - what a tremendous amount of energy built this magnificent volcanic edifice! Yet at its present rate of lava production, it might have been built in a little more than a million years.

Mauna Loa's caldera, Mokuaweoweo, is 4 miles long, 2 miles wide and 600 feet deep. Fortunately, it was mapped in 1841 by the Charles Wilkes Expedition. New pit craters have formed since that time. A comparison of that map with modern ones establishes a rate of change in the summit of a shield volcano.

A typical eruption of Mauna Loa begins in the caldera. Earth tremors, produced by rock moving beneath the surface of the summit, rattle seismometers in the Volcano Observatory 25 miles away. As magma reaches the surface, a fume cloud appears. Lava fountaining along the rift produces a »curtain of fire« that continues for hours or days. Great volumes of lava pour out, and with the pressure relieved the volcano becomes quiescent for a few hours, or two or three days. Activity resumes, this time outside the crater as a flank eruption.

Even though the lava is much more viscous than water, it may move in channels at speeds up to 25 miles per hour and travel as far as 35 miles from the vent before cooling. Upon entering the sea the lava bursts into clouds of steam. The sudden chilling of the lava shatters it into fine bits that pile up into cones of black sand, littoral cones that look like cinder cones but are nowhere near a vent. A row of littoral cones is at South Point (Ka Lae).

The road from Kilauea to South Point runs along the Koiki fault scarp that ends in the Great Crack near the sea. Another long fault scarp is at South Point where a vertical displacement of 600 feet decreases to nothing, 10 miles inland. But traced in the opposite direction, it runs 18 miles seaward onto the ocean floor.

Beyond South Point the road turns north and crosses flow after flow of recent lavas that have poured out of vents on the south rift of Mauna Loa and run down to the sea. A third great fault is at Kealakekua where the seaward side of the island slid downward to create Kealakekua Bay, now famous as the place where the British explorer, Capt. James Cook, was killed over the matter of the native Hawaiians stealing one of his ship's cutters for its coveted nails.

Hualalai

Hualalai's surface is studded with 120 cinder and spatter cones. It is entering a late stage of its eruptive cycle with its lava less rich in iron but more rich in silicon and aluminum. A crack formed on the northwest flank of Hualalai in 1800/1801 and produced the Kaupulehu flow. Since then it has not erupted.

Hualalai is older than Mauna Loa and younger than Mauna Kea, and all of them blend into saddle-shaped plateaus between them.

Mauna Kea

Mauna Kea steepens at its summit. The tallest shield rises 13,796 feet above sea level from a base almost 20,000 feet beneath the waves. Mauna Kea built its shield of basalt and then rested. But when it started up again, its chemistry had changed, its lava less fluid this time. Instead of flowing freely as before, the lava tended to pile up around the vent, steepening the summit and producing 150 cinder cones.

One of those late eruptions flowed down a valley and out into the sea to form a lava fan, Laupahoehoe. Four miles inland and near Hilo, Kolekole Stream pours over a resistant ledge and falls 412 feet into a plunge pool, a scene of beauty honored in one of Hawaii's famous songs, »Akaka Falls.«

A glacier occupying the summit of Mauna Kea during a recent ice age scratched the bedrock and piled debris into glacial moraines at an elevation of 11,000 feet. Since the latest eruptions cover parts of that moraine, it is assumed that the last major activity happened about 15,000 years ago.

The Mauna Kea summit has become an international astronomy lab, with the following telescopes in operation: two 24″ telescopes, one 2.4m-telescope (University of Hawaii), one 3m-infra-red telescope (NASA), one 3.6m-telescope (Canada-France-Hawaii), one 3.8m-infra-red telescope (United Kingdom), one 10.4m-CalTech submillimeter telescope and one 15m-James-Clerke-Maxwell multiple array telescope. In the process of being built is one 10m-William-Keck telescope, to be completed in 1991, while several other large telescopes are in the planning stage. Already, Mauna Kea hosts the greatest collection of large telescopes on the planet. There is probably no better place in the world than Mauna Kea for viewing the universe; its summit is above 96 percent of the earth's vapor, the cause of unsteady viewing at lower levels. From this vantage point you look *down* onto trade wind clouds.

Kohala

Large cinder cones dot the crest of the Kohala shield at the north end of Hawaii. The western side of this mountain is dry, with only small gulches indenting its surface. But the windward side receives abundant rain

that has formed huge sea cliffs between Waipio and Pololu valleys. The sea has cut back these long lava slopes into cliffs. Since the volcano was completed, perhaps 800,000 years ago, the rate of erosion is about 8 inches per century. It is not an alarming rate of erosion, but when you see just how far back the cliffs are truncated, you get an inkling of a magnitude of time that eludes human comprehension.

Across Alenuihaha Channel from Kohala and the Big Island looms the massive shield, Haleakala.

THE ISLAND OF MAUI

The island of Maui is two shields connected by an isthmus commonly called the »central plain.« The western volcano, the West Maui Mountain, is nearly circular in shape, covered with vegetation and heavily dissected by erosion. Valleys radiate from its summit like spokes from a giant wheel, giving the island its name, »Valley Isle.« The eastern mountain is Haleakala, 10,023 feet high, dome-shaped, and barren at the top.

The Hana region at the eastern tip of Maui is isolated from the rest of the island by steep sea cliffs over which waterfalls plunge 200 feet into the sea. Because it is »not connected« to the rest of the island, the Hana region historically is more closely related to the island of Hawaii than it is to the rest of Maui. Two hundred years ago powerful Hawaiian chiefs, including Kamehameha I, sent warriors in outrigger canoes to capture Maui.

Gaining control of »Hana-of-the-low-lying-clouds« was relatively easy for these warriors because it is separated from Hawaii by only the Alenuihaha Channel. The Hawaiians found Hana as easy to capture as the Mauians found it difficult to defend. Kamehameha succeeded in taking the entire island of Maui and eventually uniting all the islands under his rule.

A trail once ran from Hana up the east rift of Haleakala, across the crater floor and down the other side into the central valley. Remnants of the trail, alternately covered and uncovered by wind-drifted volcanic cinders and dust, still exist in the crater. Hana is now joined to the rest of Maui by a narrow winding road that makes its way along the sea cliffs.

A rift running across the floor of Haleakala's summit depression is marked by a line of colorful cinder cones. The 600-foot-high Puu o Maui is one of them. Viewed from the top of the mountain, it is not all that impressive since it is dwarfed by the immensity of the summit depression of which it is a part. But descend 3,000 feet down the Sliding Sands trail to the crater floor and you will be impressed by its size. Interesting to explore are those small volcanic features with sprightly names – Bubble Cave, Pele's Pig Pen, Bottomless Pit, Grumbling Hill and Pele's Paint Pot.

Haleakala *crater*? Oval in shape, this crater measures 3 miles by 7 miles and has the appearance of a caldera. It's called a crater but that's a misnomer. A crater is a depression at the top of a volcano formed by either explosion or collapse. There is no evidence that Haleakala's summit depression formed in either of those two ways. Extensive geologic work has shown that for a time, when volcanic activity had ceased, erosion dominated. The mountain was high enough to trap the moisture-laden trade wind clouds. Rain fell and streams began to cut channels down its slopes. Two such streams eroding their way headward created large amphitheater-like depressions near the summit of Haleakala. Ultimately these two valleys met, creating a long erosional »crater.« When volcanic activity resumed near the summit, lava poured down the stream valleys, nearly filling them. More recently, cinders, ash, volcanic bombs and spatter were blown from the numerous young vents in the crater forming multi-colored symmetrical cones. Thus this water-carved basin came to resemble a true volcanic crater.

Though dormant now, about 1790 two minor flows at lower elevations along the southwest rift zone of Haleakala reached the sea and altered the southwest coastline of Maui. Today, earthquake records indicate that internal adjustments are still taking place in the earth's crust, but at present, no volcanic activity of any form is visible in the crater. Perhaps, one day, Haleakala might erupt again.

Here at the top of Haleakala, the »House of the Sun,« the demigod Maui snared the sun, forcing it to travel slower across the sky so that his mother, Hina, would have more time for the drying of the *kapa,* or *tapa,* (bark-cloth). From this vantage point you can look far beyond the island and see the Big Island's magnificent shields – Mauna Kea, Mauna Loa and Hualalai – rising above the trade wind clouds.

Blowing up through Koolau Gap, clouds spread across Haleakala's crater floor and frequently fill the summit depression. When that happens, you can stand at the edge of the crater, with the sun behind you, and see your own shadow cast down upon the clouds and surrounded by a rainbow – the »spectre of brochen.« When you're in those clouds as you hike a trail, you're peacefully separated from the rest of the world.

The summit of the West Maui Mountain is half as high as Haleakala. Between them is the great central valley where old sand dunes have turned to stone. The dunes were formed many thousands of years ago when the sea was about 250 feet lower than it is now. Trade winds swept across broad stretches of sandy beach and piled the sand up into dunes. Vegetation anchored the dunes, and acids from plant roots changed the insoluble calcium carbonate into a soluble bicarbonate form that percolated through the dunes, cementing sand grains into a semi-solid rock.

Behind the town of Wailuku is Iao Valley. A short hike here brings you into the center of the West Maui volcano, the caldera region which has been enlarged by erosion into a great amphitheater a mile in diameter. Vertical walls are covered with vegetation, and in the deep recesses between the fin-like divides, waterfalls tumble hundreds of feet into plunge pools. Famous Iao Needle is a prominent, isolated pinnacle at the end of a ridge.

KAHOOLAWE AND LANAI

The island of Kahoolawe lies off the west coast slope of Haleakala. Dry and dusty, uninhabited Kahoolawe is in the rain shadow of Haleakala. Northwest of it is the corporately owned island of Lanai. Crescent shaped and highly eroded, Lanai's broad, low caldera is filled with pineapple, giving rise to its name »Pineapple Island.« To the north is the island of Molokai.

MOLOKAI

Molokai lies between Maui and Oahu. Rectangular in shape, 38 miles long and 10 miles wide, the »Friendly Isle« is built primarily of two shield volcanoes.

East Molokai is the younger of the two. The summit of this shield was once indented by a caldera 2 miles wide and 4 miles long. Erosion is now removing the caldera fill. The northern side of East Molokai is truncated by sea cliffs more than 3,000 feet high. So steep and abrupt are these cliffs that early workers assumed they formed because of faulting. But there's no evidence to support that theory. The great cliffs are a combination of the work of streams and the work of the sea. Stream erosion carves great valleys, and the headlands between them are eroded by the sea relentlessly carving away at the bases of the cliffs.

West Molokai is worn down into rolling hills. Red lateritic soil up to 50 feet deep covers this part of the island, indicating a long period of inactivity. Spectacular lines of parallel sand dunes run from the sea 5 miles inland across the northwestern corner of the island, reaching heights of 60 feet. Twenty-two miles across the Kaiwi Channel is the island of Oahu.

OAHU

Oahu is the summits of the Koolau and the Waianae volcanoes, connected in the Schofield Plateau. Waianae is the older of the two, crescent shaped with huge valleys on its leeward side. It was completed about 5 million years ago and for a long time was the entire island. Stream erosion carved the huge amphitheater-headed valleys of Lualualei, Makaha and Makua.

Hundreds of thousands of years later, explosions and sputterings 25 miles to the east produced the island of Koolau. Flows from it and the Waianae volcano pounded against each other and eventually joined the separate islands into one, the island of Oahu.

The Koolau range is 40 miles long and has the shape of an inverted canoe, much like that of Mauna Loa. Major volcanic activity ceased perhaps 3 million years ago and a long period of erosion followed. During that erosional period, the great valleys behind Honolulu were carved – Moanalua, Kalihi, Nuuanu, Manoa and Palolo. The heads of the valleys have enlarged into great amphitheaters as a result of the abundance of rain at higher elevations.

Erosion on the windward side of the Koolau mountain has been great enough to wear away the inter-stream divides and form »The Pali,« a long cliff of fluted columns about a 1,000 feet high. Perhaps nowhere else in the world is the power of streams to erode a basaltic shield volcano into striking forms shown so dramatically.

A flurry of volcanic activity in the late stages of Oahu's growth formed 30 cones in the Honolulu area. Diamond Head, Punchbowl and Koko Head are notable ones. These three are *tuff* cones – products of steam explosions. Each has formed near the sea where water is abundant.

Diamond Head formed 300,000 years ago, a mile offshore of Waikiki. Molten rock rising from below heated the water trapped in cracks, crevices, lava tubes and coral deposits, and built up pressure. When the pressure of the super-heated water exceeded that of the overlying burden of rock, a gigantic steam explosion blasted outward, hurling ash and dust high into the air. The rapidly expanding steam blew the magma apart into a spray of tiny fragments and droplets that hardened in the air into glassy ash particles the size of sand. When the pressure decreased, the sides of the new cone slumped, sealing off the vent. When the air cleared, the tuff ring of Diamond Head appeared. Erosional material brought down from the Koolau mountain by streams filled in the region between Diamond Head and the shore, tying it to the island. A growth of coral reef takes the brunt of the breaking waves and protects Diamond Head from erosion by the sea.

About 100,000 years later, up in the mountains behind Honolulu, lava spewed high into the air to form the cinder cone Tantalus. The two cones, Tantalus and Diamond Head, are of the same chemical composition but of quite different physical form. Black Tantalus ash spread all over the region that is now Honolulu. Foundations of modern buildings go through that layer of ash down to stronger footing on the older coral and basaltic rocks.

Coral patches are found around Oahu, and the closest to a fringing reef anywhere in Hawaii is on the windward side of the island. The reef here is made of living matter, about 80 percent plant material, 20 percent animal remains. Even though it is more plant than coral remains, it still is often called »coral« reef.

Cliffs, reefs and secondary volcanics are marks of Oahu's individuality. Eighty miles to the northwest of this island, beyond vicious Kauai Channel, is the »Garden Isle,« with its own mark of individuality, the »Little Grand Canyon.«

KAUAI

The island of Kauai is essentially a single great volcano, deeply eroded and veneered with later volcanic eruptions. The Kauai volcano rises 17,000 feet from its base on the ocean floor to its misty summit, Mount Waialeale. Its 5,148-foot cloud-shrouded peak is among the wettest places on earth, averaging 444 inches of rain a year.

Perhaps seven million years ago when the Kauai volcano was completed, a huge caldera occupied the top of the shield. As time passed, the southern side of the volcano began to collapse, forming a trough 4 miles wide, the Makaweli graben. Time after time volcanic activity in the caldera overflowed the crater rim, sending lava pouring down into the graben and out into the sea. Flowing along the western wall of the graben is Waimea Stream. Its direction does not conform to that of other streams in the region; instead it largely flows diagonally across the ancient drainage pattern, that direction being determined by structural collapse. Exposed in the walls of spectacular Waimea Canyon, often called the »Little Grand Canyon,« are horizontal flows of lava. Heavy rainfall is dissecting these flat-lying caldera rocks into sharp ridges, while chemical alteration is coloring them red, beige, ochre and green. Color and topography combine to produce a scene reminiscent of the canyon country of the western United States. And like the Grand Canyon, it is laced with trails that wind around sunlit prominences and into dark valley recesses.

Outside the caldera are ancient lava flows sloping down toward the sea at angles of 6 to 10 degrees. In the region along the northwestern side of the island are sharp, thin ridges remaining between gigantic vertical grooves. The sea has worn away at those finger-like prominences, truncating them into the Na Pali cliffs.

The privately owned island of Niihau lies near Kauai, and beyond it for the next 1,200 miles are the older islands in the Hawaiian chain – smaller, worn-down islands that mark the summits of shields riding the Pacific plate to the northwest, destined to be reincorporated into the mantle of the earth.

ISLAND HISTORY: ATTRACTING THE SEEKERS by Edward Joesting

The first settlers to step onto the shores of the Hawaiian Islands sailed up from the south, from the Marquesas Islands, across the equator into the northern latitudes of the Pacific Ocean. When the discoverers came ashore around 500 A.D., more than 2,000 miles of open ocean lay between them and their former homes.

The voyaging canoes the Marquesans traveled in were double-hulled, equipped with a woven mat sail, and perhaps 40 feet in length. The canoes could hold 40 or 50 paddlers, along with the plants and animals needed to sustain life in a new land.

The intrepid Marquesans were part of a greater Polynesian race which peopled South Pacific islands from New Zealand in the west to Easter Island in the east. The discovery of Hawaii marked the northern apex of what would become known as the Polynesian triangle. By 800 A.D. the Hawaiian Islands were well populated.

What drove the Marquesans to seek new homes is not known, although evidence from ancient Marquesan civilization indicates overpopulation in those islands. As a result, wars and famine could have driven groups of people to set forth, hoping to discover islands where fear of starvation and sudden death would not dominate their lives.

During the early centuries, from the time of the first Hawaii settlement until about 1100 A.D., fertile, well-watered windward lands were plentiful and crops were abundant. Fishing was safe and easy in coastal waters protected by coral reefs. Government was by local chiefs, family units were common, and restrictions were not severe.

But such ideal conditions resulted in an increased population. Gradually it became necessary to establish more rules to maintain an ordered society. In the process, cleavage between commoners and chiefs became more marked. Political rivalries became more sensitive, and persons became specialized in their occupations. With the increased population, less desirable lands had to be put into use. This situation continued until about 1450 A.D.

Around that time a new era evolved as the population started on a dramatic upward spiral, resulting in intense pressure to make the land produce the most food possible. Chiefs took on greater degrees of sanctity. Rivalries became sharper, precious land was often disputed and wars were more frequent.

The Hawaiians had no written language, but Hawaiian oral history recounts that in about 1450 a Tahitian chief named Paao arrived in the Islands. Paao was shocked by the informality of the Hawaiians and he was able to impose new, rigid rules on Island society. Fear now marked the increasingly ritualized relationships between commoners and chiefs. Lineage was given new importance. Religious observances became more formalized, and the practice of human sacrifices is believed to date from the time of Paao.

During this same period, around 1450, a chief named Umi became the supreme ruler of the island of Hawaii. Umi was renowned as an organizer, and perhaps it was during his time that the extensive mountain slopes along the Kona Coast were arranged into four zones according to elevation so crops could be grown in the environment best suited for them. Fish were raised for food within rock wall enclosures that encircled sections of shallow shoreline. In all of Polynesia, fishponds were developed only in Hawaii. Clearly, producing enough food had become critical.

This was the condition of Hawaiian society when Capt. James Cook, the renowned English explorer, discovered the Hawaiian Islands for the Western world. James Cook first sighted the Islands, which he named the Sandwich Islands in honor of his patron Lord Sandwich, in January 1778. He was sailing north from Tahiti, toward the Arctic Sea, hoping to find a Northwest Passage which would lead above the North American continent into the Atlantic Ocean. To Cook's amazement he came on the high islands of Hawaii.

Cook paused briefly at Kauai and Niihau to take on provisions, then continued north on his mission. Less than a year later he was back in the Hawaiian Islands after unsuccessfully seeking the Northwest Passage. He sought a harbor where he could safely repair his ships and replenish his food supplies. Kealakekua Bay, on the island of Hawaii, was the best bay Cook could find and it was on the rocky shore there that Cook met his death in a skirmish with the Hawaiians over the return of a stolen cutter.

Cook's ships again sailed north after the tragedy, and again failing to find a Northwest Passage, returned to England by way of Canton, China, and the Cape of Good Hope. In Hawaii, the rulers continued their wars, remembering with longing Cook's impressive ships and death-dealing weapons which could quickly have given any chief victory over his rivals.

The Cook expedition into the Pacific brought deep changes to isolated Hawaii. While on the Northwest Coast of the American continent, Cook's crew took aboard sea otter pelts and in Canton, China, these furs were sold at enormous profits. Spurred on by the hope of profits, Nathaniel Portlock and George Dixon, both of whom had served with Cook, hastened back to the Northwest Coast to take on a cargo of furs. Portlock and Dixon knew that Hawaii was invaluable as a place to stop for rest and supplies on their long voyage across the Pacific and they brought their two ships to Hawaii in 1786. From then on not a single year would pass without the appearance of Western ships in Hawaiian waters.

The Hawaiian ruler most adept at grasping Western ways was the high chief Kamehameha on the island of Hawaii. He acquired a greater collection of firearms from visiting ships than his rivals and induced Westerners who knew how to use them to stay as advisers. By 1795 Kamehameha had conquered all the Islands except Kauai and Niihau. Two attempts to add these islands to his realm failed, in 1796 because of a storm in the Kauai Channel, and in 1804 because of a cholera epidemic that virtually destroyed his army. Finally, in 1810, Kaumualii, the king of Kauai, peacefully became a tributary ruler under Kamehameha, and the unification of the Hawaiian Islands was complete.

Weapons were not the only death-dealing importation of Western man. Many diseases to which the Hawaiians had no immunity made deadly inroads in the Hawaiian population. Cook's men had infected the natives with venereal diseases and other maladies soon followed. Smallpox and bubonic plague caused thousands of deaths, while ailments minor to Western man proved fatal to Hawaiians. Over the years the consistent killer of Islanders proved to be tuberculosis.

Provisioning ships on Pacific crossings provided a meager source of income, but the discovery of sandalwood and the realization of its value to the Chinese created a new interest in Hawaii for merchant-captains. The fragrant heartwood of the sandalwood tree was used by the Chinese to make chests, boxes, and fans, while the shavings were burned as incense. The demand for the wood was so great and the luxuries which could be bought with the proceeds so tempting that many chiefs ordered commoners into the wet, cold mountains to cut the wood. Cutting and carrying the wood to the shore was so exhausting that many died, another cause for the decrease in numbers of the Hawaiian race.

Kamehameha, the unifier of the Islands, died in 1819 and the passing of that strong ruler signaled extensive changes. Kamehameha had continued to enforce the ancient *kapu* (taboo) system, the complex set of rules which was the fabric of order in Hawaiian society. Shortly after the old ruler died, his son, Kamehameha II, and a widow, Kaahumanu, who had become premier of the kingdom, declared that the old system was dead. The demise of the intricate kapu system left a vacuum in the lives of the Hawaiians.

As these changes were occurring, a group of Protestant missionaries from New England was sailing for the Islands. Driven by a new missionary awareness, which had its origins in Europe and England, the missionaries felt conscience-bound to carry the doctrines of the Bible to the heathen. When they arrived in Hawaii on March 30, 1820, they learned that the demise of the old system had opened the way for Christianity. More missionaries arrived over the years and the dedication of these men and women left an impression on the Islands which remains today.

Another event occurred in 1819 which would also have long-ranging effects on Hawaii. Two New England whaling vessels, pushing ever farther in their search for diminishing schools of whales, came to anchor in Kealakekua Bay. News of their good luck in taking whales in Island waters soon spread and other vessels quickly followed them into the North Pacific. The strategic location of the Islands brought hundreds of ships to Hawaiian ports, seeking supplies, sending crews ashore on leave, and transshipping whale oil and bone to home ports.

The whalers were mostly from New England ports, but there were also English ships and occasionally visitors from France, Germany and the Scandinavian countries. While the English were early and influential in Hawaii, European wars and wars with the U.S. reduced the number of British vessels reaching the Pacific.

Russian exploring expeditions, often captained by Prussians or Germans, periodically stopped in Hawaiian ports. The first, under A. J. von Krusenstern, had arrived in 1804. The Russian-American Company, which was well established in Alaska by the early 1800s, had made in ill-advised attempt to form an alliance with King Kaumualii of Kauai in 1816–1817. Dr. Georg Scheffer, who headed this attempt, was soon driven from the Islands and his actions were disavowed by the Russian-American Company.

Through the first half of the 19th century the United States and England, and to a lesser degree France, vied for power in Hawaii. The rulers of Hawaii had been impressed with the English, beginning with James Cook and followed by explorers like George Vancouver, and for a time the Hawaiians even considered themselves under the protection of England. Hawaiian chiefs adopted English names, many assuming the name George, after King George III. In 1824 King Kamehameha II, his queen, and a company of Hawaiian royalty visited England. Both the king and queen died of measels while in London. During this time of sorrow the helpfulness of the British government, specifically in carrying the royal remains back to Hawaii aboard a warship, enhanced respect for England.

Foreign powers were rarely so considerate toward the Hawaiian government. On two occasions in 1826, U.S. warships arrived in Hawaii to forcefully remind the chiefs that their debts to U.S. merchants were delinquent and payment was expected. In 1839 and again in 1849 French warships arrived demanding that a list of conditions be met or war would follow. In the course of events the French destroyed the fort at Honolulu, the king's yacht was stolen, and a government deposit of $ 20,000 never returned. In 1843 a British captain threatened to open fire on Honolulu if his demands were not met. A frustrated Hawaiian government ceded the Islands to England and they remained under the British flag for five months.

In spite of such interferences from the great powers of the world, the Hawaiian monarchy managed not only to survive, but to progress. Under American tutelage the government moved cautiously toward a representative form of government. In 1840 a constitution laid down a plan of government. It provided for an elected House of Representatives, which gave the common people a voice in government for the first time, and provided for a Supreme Court. In 1852 a revised constitution included a bill of rights and divided government into legislative, executive and judicial branches. The king remained the supreme executive.

Ever since Westerners had settled in the Islands there had been conflicting concepts of land ownership. In ancient times the king had owned all land, parceling out sections to loyal chiefs who held it at the will of the king. As Western influence became stronger there was increasing dissatisfaction with the system. Westerners wanted full and outright ownership of land. After various attempts at solutions, a *mahele,* or division of the lands, was undertaken. In 1848 chiefs and commoners were given the right to claim full title to lands they had historically occupied. The king retained a vast amount of land as property of the Crown and a large amount of land went to the government. The mahele was a giant step in the Westernizing of Hawaii.

Through these changes the descendants of the first Kamehameha continued to rule Hawaii. Kamehameha III ascended the throne in 1825 at the age of 11. His ruling years witnessed the intervention of foreign powers and the mahele. Kamehameha IV followed in 1854. He married Emma Rooke and the two brought the English Episcopal Church to Hawaii.

Supplying whaling vessels was the first substantial source of income the Islands knew. Ships stopped at all the major islands, but Honolulu and Lahaina, Maui, were the leading ports. For the 12 years from 1843 through 1854 an average of 419 whalers stopped at the Islands each year. In landlocked Honolulu Harbor, ships had the luxury of tying up at a pier. At Lahaina, ships anchored in the roads and supplies had to be rowed to and from the shore.

Vessels took on barrels of salt pork and beef, potatoes, melons, fresh vegetables, and tethered sheep, goats and cattle on deck to be slaughtered later at sea. Sailors, pent up for months in crowded quarters, spilled into towns where sometimes the outnumbered police could do little to control them.

While Hawaii was enjoying the profits and suffering the problems of visiting whalers, California was changing from a thinly populated near-wilderness to a land crowded with boisterous gold-seekers. Gold was discovered in California in 1848 and Honolulu, the closest civilized town, was the first outside place to hear the news. Many Islanders left to seek their fortunes in the gold fields. Shops in Honolulu were stripped of merchandise which was sold at enormous profit in California. In winter, gold-seekers came to Hawaii to escape the rain and snow. In 1850 California was admitted as a state of the United States.

So, suddenly the U.S. was established on the West Coast of North America, making it by far the closest major power to Hawaii. With the great majority of the whalers coming from the U.S. and the new importance of California as a market for Hawaiian produce, Hawaii became firmly tied economically to the U.S.

In December 1872 Kamehameha V lay dying and a final, futile effort was made to get him to name a successor. A lifelong bachelor, the king had no heir. It was then up to the Legislature to name a new ruler. The person chosen was William Lunalilo, a man of immense popularity, but with little experience or aptitude for the job. King Lunalilo died less than 13 months after his election, without an heir. So the election process was repeated in 1874 with the congenial David Kalakaua emerging the victor over Queen dowager Emma.

A dozen years before Kalakaua became king the whaling business had come to a virtual halt. With the discovery of petroleum, its by-product kerosene replaced whale oil as a fuel for lamps. The number of visiting whaling ships, so long Hawaii's main source of income, suddenly and drastically declined.

As whaling faded, the growing and milling of sugar cane had gotten enough of a start to give promise of filling the economic void. The first successful plantation had been founded in 1835 at Koloa on Kauai and the industry had grown through trial and error over the years.

In 1874, the year of Kalakaua's election, sugar fields covered large areas on the major islands. A continuing problem, however, was the lack of a stable market for sugar and there was much discussion about a reciprocity treaty with the United States. Such a treaty would allow sugar to enter the U.S. duty free, and in return, U.S. goods would enter the Islands duty free.

The U.S. agreed to a reciprocity treaty in 1876, an event that marks a turning point in modern Hawaiian history. The assurance of a market for sugar brought an optimism which resulted in a flow of investment money into Hawaii. In 1875, the year before the reciprocity treaty, 25 million pounds of sugar were exported. Ten years later, more than 171 million pounds of sugar were exported.

For almost a century sugar would so dominate Hawaii's economy that all business prospered or declined in step with it. Sugar dictated shipping schedules, determined where towns would be located and set the very pace of life. Sugar was also a labor-intensive business and this focused attention on Hawaii's population, which had been declining ever since the coming of Western man. The danger was frighteningly clear. Hawaii's sugar industry was in jeopardy. Indeed, the existence of Hawaii as a nation was threatened.

In addressing the opening of the Legislature in 1874, King Kalakaua stated that his greatest concern was the Islands' declining population. He called on the lawmakers »to direct your earnest attention« to the matter. By 1876 the population had dropped to an all-time low of 54,000, of which about 90 percent were Hawaiians or Part-Hawaiians. At the time of James Cook's arrival, nearly 100 years earlier, the estimated population of the Islands was about 300,000.

The government's dual hope was to increase the population by bringing other Polynesian peoples to Hawaii and at the same time find workers for the plantations. It would have been ideal if the two objectives could have been combined, but it was impossible. The Polynesians who eventually came to Hawaii were a success neither as workers nor as permanent residents. The first small start at importing workers had taken place much earlier, in 1852, when a group of Chinese arrived. Chinese were anxious to come and more were brought as the need arose.

Bringing Chinese was the easiest answer, but by 1876 there were fears among some that the Chinese might eventually dominate the Islands through sheer numbers. It was believed workers from Western nations would reinforce Western ideas, so Europeans were sought and brought to Hawaii. The largest number came from the Portuguese islands of Madeira and Azore. Others came from Norway, Germany, Sweden and Russia. Westerners, however, were not willing to come under the same conditions as the Chinese; they wanted to bring their families with them, for example, and the cost, time and trouble added up to more than the government or the planters wanted to pay.

In desperation the planters turned again to the Chinese, who were always quickly available. The fear of Chinese dominance, however, did not disappear and workers were sought from other places. At last Japan was again considered as a major source, seeing also that the first Japanese, who arrived »inofficially« in 1868, had turned out to be able workers. Kalakaua visited Japan during his 1881 world tour and the Hawaiian king and Japanese officials got along well. But the Japanese government was extremely protective of its citizens and time-consuming negotiations followed. Only after official visits, proper assurances and numerous details had been formalized, did the Japanese government allow the new first emigrants to leave Japan. In February 1885, the ship *City of Tokio* arrived in Hawaii with 944 aboard.

The Japanese workers were carefully screened, especially during the first years, as to suitability for field work, and plantation managers generally approved of them. At the end of 1894 there were 20,271 in the Islands and they composed about 20 percent of Hawaii's population. The first hope, securing Polynesians to bolster the Hawaiian race, had not been accomplished, but the second, recruiting workers, had been achieved.

Plantation laborers were brought to Hawaii on a contract basis. Contracts called for immigrants to work for a specified number of years, usually three, at wages that usually increased at the end of the first and second years. Working hours, housing and the right to buy food from the plantation were often specified in the contracts.

Plantation work was terribly hard and opportunities for promotion small, so many workers did not renew their contracts when they expired. While some workers returned to their homelands with their savings, many chose to remain in the Islands, often opening small businesses of their own. This turnover resulted in a continuing flow of new immigrant workers into the Islands.

While the problem of finding workers appeared solved, a gap was widening between the Kalakaua government and Island businessmen. The complaints of the businessmen centered on the extravagance and ostentation of the Kalakaua regime. The opinions of the businessmen were uncompromising, and the attitude of Kalakaua and his followers was one of disinterest toward criticism.

In 1887 a confrontation took place. The events which led up to the crisis included the taking of a bribe by Kalakaua and an attempt to interfere in the affairs of Samoa. After a noisy, emotional public meeting on June 30, 1887, Kalakaua was called on by a delegation of businessmen who presented a list of demands. Kalakaua agreed to the demands and the monarchy was shorn of much of its power.

While the Kalakaua regime and the business community kept a wary eye on each other, still other problems had to be faced. A long-standing, nagging concern was transportation between the major islands and Honolulu. Before Cook, the Hawaiians had traveled in outrigger canoes. Later, small schooners plied the channels, carrying cargo and people whenever it was profitable. When sugar plantations became established on Maui, Kauai and Hawaii, transportation to Honolulu became vital, because people and cargoes of sugar had to be moved on some kind of a schedule. As a solution, some plantations ran their own schooners to Honolulu.

With the coming of steamships, crossing channels was quicker and on schedule, but the hazards of reefs and the difficulties of anchoring offshore and ferrying cargo and passengers to and from the beach remained unchanged. Ships were still ripped open on coral reefs and driven ashore by sudden changes in wind. Honolulu continued to be the only protected harbor in the Islands. The costs of harbor improvements were enormous and could not be met unless the Islands became a U.S. possession and money was made available by the federal government.

In 1890 Kalakaua's health had deteriorated and in late November that year he was taken to the cooler climate of California aboard the USS *Charleston.* In early January 1891 Kalakaua suffered a stroke and on January 20 he died in San Francisco. His body was carried back to Hawaii on the same ship that had taken him away. The people of the Islands were unaware of his death until they saw the black-draped ship with a Hawaiian flag at half-mast pass Diamond Head on its way to Honolulu Harbor.

During the absence of Kalakaua, his sister Liliuokalani, heiress apparent, had been appointed to act as regent. On the day Kalakaua's body was returned to Hawaii, Liliuokalani took the oath to uphold the constitution and became the new ruler of Hawaii. The heralds of the kingdom made the news known through the streets of Honolulu.

Liliuokalani had been outspoken in criticizing those who had opposed her brother. The 52-year-old queen also felt her brother had been weak in dealing with his opposition and she was particularly upset with the restrictions that had been forced on the monarchy in 1887.

By the end of 1892, relations had deteriorated between the queen and a substantial part of the community. In January 1893 the queen brought matters to a head when she announced her intention to arbitrarily put a new constitution into effect. She was stymied in her attempt, however, by frightened cabinet members who refused to sign the document. Her opponents considered this action by Liliuokalani her final misdeed and on January 17 a small group of men gathered at the government office building to proclaim that the monarchy was deposed and a provisional government was established. It was a near-bloodless revolution. Only one shot was fired and one man wounded.

Many of the men involved in the overthrow were American citizens or had strong ties with the U.S. Some expected the Islands would quickly be annexed by the U.S. This was not to be the case. There were hearings and lengthy debates over whether the revolt had been justified or not. For five years the Islands functioned as a republic until finally, in 1898, Congress annexed Hawaii. Two years later, Hawaii officially became a Territory.

As a territory of the United States the Hawaiian Islands experienced gentle but far-reaching changes. While it may have been aggravating to have important decisions such as the appointing of judges and the naming of a governor made in far-off Washington, D.C., there were also benefits such as federal funds to build roads, bridges, breakwaters, health facilities and harbors. Sanford Dole, who had served as president of the republic, was appointed Hawaii's first governor. As a territory, the Islands were allowed to elect a delegate, who would be a non-voting member of Congress.

Territorial status also brought investment capital to the Islands because people across the Mainland believed the U.S. presence meant security. Money became available for the improvement of sugar plantations, and land values soared. Slowly military bases were built at Pearl Harbor and eventually at Schofield Plateau in central Oahu. Such installations meant federal payrolls, a welcomed addition to Island income.

During this same period, pineapple was being successfully grown and canned. James Dole, a young man who was a distant relative of Sanford Dole, came to Hawaii from New England in 1899 and planted pineapple on the upper plateau of Oahu. The canned fruit became popular across the U.S. and in Europe. Hawaii became internationally known as the source of pineapple.

Japanese continued to come to the Islands, still much in demand as workers in the sugar and pineapple fields. Among the new races to arrive were Filipinos and Koreans. The 1910 census showed 79,700 Japanese, 44,000 Caucasians, 38,500 Hawaiians and Part-Hawaiians, 21,700 Chinese, 4,500 Koreans and 2,400 Filipinos. The total population in that year was 192,000.

When World War I began, the Hawaiian Islands were about as far from the fighting as it was possible to be. For many years preceeding the war, men of British, German and American ancestry had controlled Island business and had gotten along well. During the first years of the war, relationships continued on a reasonably friendly basis, but as the European conflict became more terrible, emotions in Hawaii became less tolerant. Hackfeld and Company, German-controlled and the largest company in the Islands, was taken over by order of the U.S. government and sold to American interests. Suspicion and finally hysteria took hold as the war progressed. Many persons with German names were hounded from the Islands and evidence of German influence in Hawaii virtually disappeared.

During the 1920s the sugar and pineapple industries prospered while federal spending added to Hawaii's income. The first faint beginnings of a tourist industry were appearing. Transportation between the major islands vastly improved and travel to the mainland U.S. aboard ocean liners was pleasant and frequent. Since 1902 a cable link with San Francisco had kept Hawaii in instant touch with the rest of the world.

In 1920 Hawaii was an agricultural place, 64 percent of the population was rural, and the only sizable city was Honolulu. On the plantations the workers were mostly first-generation immigrants. There were a few strikes or work-stoppages for higher wages by workers during the 1920s and 1930s, organized along racial lines, but largely unsuccessful. The days of significant power for the labor unions would not come until after World War II. In the meantime, the children of immigrants were attending public schools where they were learning the American system and its possibilities. As adults, many would achieve success far beyond their youthful expectations.

The end of the 1920s brought the Great Depression with its worldwide repercussions. In Hawaii, unemployment increased and caused concern, but the Islands suffered less than most other places. Hawaii had record sugar production during the first few years of the Depression and, although prices dropped, the tonnage of sugar sold was greater than at any previous time. Construction of military installations continued undiminished throughout the Depression, a vital addition to Hawaii's economic well-being. Hurt most by the Depression was the pineapple industry; because pineapple was a luxury food, sales declined.

Throughout the 1930s construction continued at Pearl Harbor, the foremost U.S. naval base in the Pacific, and on the vast army base at Schofield Barracks. Each year the number of armed forces personnel stationed in Hawaii increased. By 1930 their number reached 18,900, and by 1940 the total was 30,000.

The attack by the Japanese on Pearl Harbor on the morning of December 7, 1941, not only brought the United States into World War II, but marked the beginning of profound changes for Hawaii. For six months after the attack, the Islands awaited further attacks or even invasion by the Japanese. Only after the U.S. victory at Midway could Islanders rest easier.

During World War II the Hawaiian Islands were the staging point for military operations throughout the broad Pacific and hundreds of thousands of service men and women stopped at the Islands. Long dominated by agriculture, Hawaii was suddenly turned into an armed bastion. Never before had there been so many people or such publicity.

After the surrender of Japan in August 1945 the men and machines of war departed and Hawaii struggled to return to a civilian life. But things would never be the same. The first demonstration of change came in 1946 with a massive strike by workers on the sugar plantations. The unions, which had been weak before the war, had organized behind able leadership, and the 79-day strike of 1946 ended with workers achieving substantial gains in wages and benefits. In 1949 there was a dock strike, particularly difficult for a community so dependent on ocean shipping. Again, the union made substantial wage gains.

Other changes were evolving. Many of the children of immigrants served in the armed forces, and after the war the federal government passed legislation providing financial support for those wanting to continue their education. Many received excellent schooling and became prominent in the professions. Filled with confidence, these young men, many of them second-generation Japanese, were determined to become a political force in Hawaii.

In 1954 these newcomers won a political victory of unexpected proportions. The winners were nearly all Democrats, the party which had been a minority to the dominant Republicans since the early days of the Territory. The new Democrats opened the political process to more people than ever before and today they remain the clearly dominant power in the Islands.

Since early territorial days there had been voices calling for the admission of the Islands as a full-fledged state of the Union. For years this was routinely brought up by the Hawaiian delegate to Congress without any expectation of it being taken seriously. The loyal role Islanders played during World War II brought more immediacy to the question and the idea was promoted vigorously by Islanders and supporters across the Mainland.

After tireless efforts, success was finally achieved in March 1959 when Congress voted acceptance of Hawaii as a state. Later President Dwight D. Eisenhower approved the action and the people of the Islands voted their overwhelming agreement. It was the happy ending of a long and weary struggle for many people. Hawaii could now elect its own governor and William Quinn, Hawaii's last appointed governor, became the first elected governor.

Statehood brought tremendous publicity to Hawaii and businessmen in the U.S. and foreign countries sought investment opportunities in the Islands. Quite by coincidence, the year 1959 also brought large jet airplanes to Hawaii. These planes, a revolution in transportation, made it possible for mass movement of people at low fares. The business of tourism boomed beyond the highest expectations.

Tourism spread beyond well-known Waikiki to the other islands, where large sections of land changed in appearance as high-rise hotels rose behind previously little known beaches. By the mid-1970s this new industry pushed the traditional agricultural crops of sugar and pineapple into secondary roles.

The tourist industry continued to grow at a phenomenal rate. The accessibility of Hawaii, the temperate climate and the beauty of its beaches and mountains attracted many persons; some decided to stay and make the Islands their home. In 1960 the population of the Islands was 633,000 and by 1985 that number had reached 1,054,000.

For decades after its discovery by James Cook, Hawaii remained a distant and exotic place. Then, over the generations, merchants, missionaries, planters, laborers, military people and tourist entrepreneurs came to the Islands. They have come from every continent to join the native Hawaiians, and the modern community which has emerged is the most cosmopolitan in the world. Hawaii's two official languages are English and Hawaiian, but many others are heard in the Islands. Today this vigorous society remains Hawaii's greatest asset.

Encouraged by its two round trips to Tahiti in 1976 and 1980, the *Hokule'a*, a double-hulled voyaging canoe built in Hawaii, set sail again in July 1985 under the command of navigator Nainoa Thompson. Its two-year, 13,000-mile Voyage of Rediscovery stretched from Hawaii to Tahiti, to the Cook Islands, and to New Zealand – and back via Tonga, Samoa, Cook Islands, Tahiti and the Tuamotus Islands.

Hawaiian woman pounding *kapa*, or tapa, durable bark-cloth.

Hookupu – a gift, or offering – at Hale O Keawe heiau in Pu'uhonua O Honaunau National Historic Park. Hookupu can be any kind of an offering (such as food), but it is often a symbolic gift of a stone wrapped in *ti* leaves. It is still common to find such hookupu at the many heiau throughout the Islands.

Although they had no written language, the ancient Hawaiians carved pictures into rock with stone tools. Today we call the stone drawings petroglyphs.

The town of Lahaina on Maui was once a center of ancient Hawaiian culture and the home of important high chiefs of Maui, such as Kakaalaneo and Kahekili, and, later, the residence of Kamehameha I and the site of Hawaii's first royal palace. Missionaries from New England found rich grounds for their activities here, and Lahaina also became the Pacific's »whaling capital« in the 1840s and 1850s. In peak times up to 550 ships anchored offshore. When the whaling trade faded, sugar cane planters arrived.

Pioneer Inn, built in 1901, the brig *Carthaginian*, a 1920s schooner decked out as a 19th-century brig, the old mission houses, the 1850s courthouse and the notorious historic Hale Pa'ahao prison are all reminders of those turbulent times.

▷

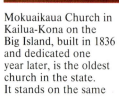

Mokuaikaua Church in Kailua-Kona on the Big Island, built in 1836 and dedicated one year later, is the oldest church in the state. It stands on the same ground where the first Christian church was built by Protestant missionaries in 1820.

St. Benedict's Church in Honaunau on the Kona coast of the Big Island, often called »Painted Church,« was built and painted by Father John Berchmans Velghe, a Belgian priest who came to Hawaii in 1899.

Lanakila Ihi'ihi O Iehova Ona Kaua Congregational Church on the Keanae peninsula on Maui's Hana coast, amidst coconut palms and taro fields, was established by missionaries in 1860.

This temple is a replica of the famous Byodo-In Temple of Kyoto, Japan. Set in a traditional Japanese garden, it is the centerpiece of the Valley of the Temples cemetery on the windward side of Oahu.

The contemplative influence of Buddhism affects the lives of many Maui residents today. To mark the 100th anniversary of the arrival of the first Japanese plantation workers on Maui, this bronze Buddha, a replica of the Daibutsu (Great Buddha) in Kamakura, Japan, was unveiled in the Lahaina Jodo Mission in 1968.

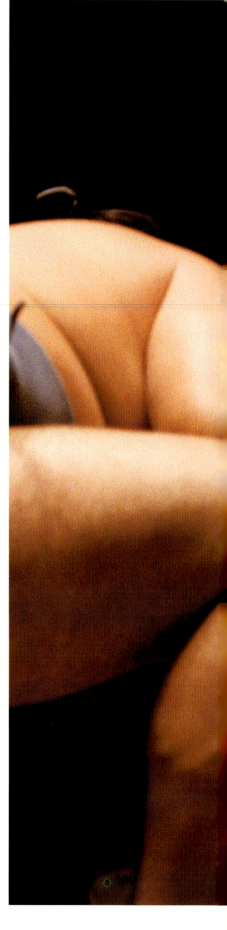

Born in 1885, Mrs. Haru Kadotani of Lahaina strums a tune on the *samisen,* a sweet-toned Japanese musical instrument.

The last bout of Hawaiian Sumo wrestling champion Takamiyama (Jesse Kuhaulua), against Japanese opponent

Masudayama on June 3, 1984, at the 8th U.S.-Japan Goodwill Sumo Tournament in Honolulu.

A festival at the
Bishop Museum in
Honolulu features
music and dance for
people of all ages
and ethnic backgrounds,
along with
demonstrations on
Island arts and crafts.
Bernice Pauahi Bishop
Museum, founded in
1899, is considered one
of the most important
museums in the United
States. It preserves
famous collections
of Hawaiian and
Polynesian cultural
items, as well as
treasures of
anthropology and
natural history.

Each November,
children of Maui gather
to celebrate »Na Mele O
Maui« (The Songs of
Maui) festival.
»Tiny« Malaikini, who
operates tours of
Hana and surrounding
areas in a minibus,
was nicknamed by
movie star Susan
Hayward when he
served as her
bodyguard on Maui in
the early 1950s. His real
name is Viewed.

Members of the Chinese community in Hawaii have doubtless achieved the highest per capita accumulation of material wealth compared to any other immigrant labor group, partly because of their longer residence on the Islands. Probably less public attention has been directed to them, however, either locally or on the Mainland, than to the achievements of the Japanese. In the early 1970s investment firms and wealthy individuals in Japan purchased many of the largest and most famous hotels and tourist facilities in Waikiki and on the other islands. The deals were welcomed at the time by many local business interests, but almost immediately drew strong resistance from those who claimed that such foreign investment would result in preferential treatment of Japanese. This contention, while typical of the charges of ethnic discrimination, has not thus far been confirmed. Islanders, as well as visitors, however, probably need to be reminded from time to time that there is no more justification for accepting the recent stereotype that »Orientals have taken over Hawaii« than for believing the earlier one, still current in some quarters, that »Hawaii is owned and controlled, lock, stock and barrel, by haoles.«

The 1977 survey likewise indicates that, dispite substantial differences in the median annual family incomes among the various ethnic groups, from the highest of $ 21,237 by Chinese to the lowest of $ 8,903 by Samoans, all nine groups except Samoans had some representatives in all income classes from the lowest of »under $ 5,000« to the highest of »$ 25,000 or over.« Stated somewhat differently, Chinese had the highest proportion of families receiving incomes in the top income class (35 percent), Samoans had none in that class and Puerto Ricans could report only 4.2 percent.

Individuals from the immigrant labor groups had been automatically excluded from the more prestigious and financially remunerative professions or managerial occupations until they could satisfy the basic educational and experiential requirements within these fields. And it was not until the middle of the 20th century that such facilities were available in Hawaii or within the possible grasp of labor immigrants or their children. According to official sources, haoles have continued to report higher than average proportions of their employed males in both professional and managerial occupations. Yet by 1950 three of the major ethnic groups from the Orient were also highly represented in such preferred occupations: Chinese as accountants, dentists, designers, civil engineers, pharmacists, retail and wholesale tradesmen and physicians and surgeons; Japanese as dentists, photographers and managers of construction firms; and Koreans as art-ists, clergymen, designers, pharmacists and welfare workers. It was also significant, however, that more recently the smaller immigrant groups such as Filipinos, Portuguese, Puerto Ricans and Southeast Asians have penetrated professional fields for which they had an interest because of their particular cultural heritage.

There is, of course, no simple solution to the dilemma of providing equal opportunity for all who may be qualified in a world with only limited laurels and rewards. The conciliation of conflicting claims for recognition and status – always difficult in a society professing democratic principles – has become even more acute with the arrival of new claimants for higher professional status on the basis of education or experience, for example, in the Philippines, Hong Kong, or elsewhere in Asia or Europe. That task of reconciling Hawaii's own residents and the continuing flow of visitors from the outside to the stark realities, as well as the possibilities, of life on such islands should be a central challenge for educators in Hawaii for many years to come.

A second dominant issue on Hawaii's agenda during the past hundred years, especially since these Islands were incorporated as a state of the United States in 1959, has centered on the dilemma of whether to be one united or several distinctive people. This question still remains partially unresolved and may properly be conceived as an Island variant of »An American Dilemma,« as Gunnar Myrdal phrased it.

About a century ago, in 1884, the residents of these islands were roughly divided, half and half, between Polynesian Islanders and eight other separate ethnic groups still recognized in the government census today. And the policy of straddling this issue, at least in official publications, has continued down to the present in deference to the division in public sentiment. Under the native monarchy, the official emphasis was naturally in support of identification by newcomers with Hawaiian goals, including miscegenation to help restore the rapidly depleting indigenous population. Further immigration of Chinese laborers was opposed by King Kamehameha IV, among others on grounds of their assumed failure to assist in this respect, while immigration from Japan was basically approved because of their presumably being »cognate« with Hawaiians and therefore likely to amalgamate.

The readiness of British and other European and American sailors and tradesmen to assist in the rehabilitation of the Hawaiian population had been noted soon after Capt. Cook's discovery of the Islands, and 983 Part-Hawaiians were already noted in the census of

1853. It is almost certain, however, that included among the 70,036 Hawaiians recorded in this census was a considerable, although unknown, number of »mixed bloods« who had been incorporated into their mother's family and nurtured like other Hawaiians. Until 1930 the persistence in census enumerations of a high proportion of »pure« Hawaiians, contrasting with a slower increase of Part-Hawaiians over the decades since 1853, would be wholly consistent with the strongly entrenched tradition of Polynesian hospitality. It was not until 1930 that the census count of Part-Hawaiians (28,224) exceeded that of »pure« Hawaiians (22,636). The ratio of Part-Hawaiians to »pure« Hawaiians recorded by a state survey in 1982 was 20 to 1 and may have been considerably higher.

Among the interesting and surprising anomalies that have appeared in Hawaii's multiracial experience is today's unprecedented sense of racial and cultural consciousness among many Hawaiians. Hawaiians had long – certainly since Capt. Cook and his three ships appeared on their seas – been keenly aware of themselves and their customs as being quite separate and different from those of the haoles. While fully aware of how sharply they and their ways stood out in contrast with the strangers and their unusual practices, Hawaiians have spontaneously maintained their deeply ingrained folkways of hospitality and concern for strangers.

Most notably since the late 1960s, virtually all the people of these islands – perhaps most markedly so the Hawaiians – have responded in one way or another to the message carried in newspapers and television of vigorous protest among the so-called minorities. Certainly all the various ethnic groups in Hawaii, including both haoles and Hawaiians, can conceive of themselves as one of the Islands' minorities and as having been abused or discriminated against to some degree. The loss of their sovereignty as an independent nation, following the revolution of 1893 and annexation by the U.S. five years later, was a serious affront to native Hawaiian pride and collective confidence, but it was not until the greater part of the succeeding century had passed that the Hawaiians had become sufficiently aroused by the injustice of those events to register any significant protest. In Alaska and on the Mainland, the granting of restitution for the loss of lands and special hunting and fishing rights to Indians and Eskimo people by the U.S. federal government provoked similar claims by Hawaiians for Crown lands, of which they had presumably been deprived by the revolution in 1893. This request for economic reparations comes from the ethnic community least disposed by their traditional values to measure worth in terms of money. The reparations movement has been promoted primarily by those Hawaiians who have most thoroughly and unconsciously assimilated Western, competitive values. Other immigrant communities, including late-coming haoles, have voiced resentments for the inequalities they have experienced, but generally with no greater vigor than have the Hawaiians.

Despite the misunderstandings and confrontations likely to occur between individuals from several contrasting cultural and linguistic groups living and working in close proximity to each other, there has been relatively little tension and much less overt violence among these groups throughout the period of major contact. Bickerings and altercations, of course, have occurred from time to time between individuals of diverse tongues and cultures, but violence between groups has been rare. The working policy has been one of »live and let live,« even during periods of class and national crisis such as work-stoppages or international warfare.

Also, the lines between the ethnic groups in Hawaii have been crossed or maintained over the years by out-group or in-group marriages or miscegenation. Marriage statistics reflect the extent to which this *laissez faire* policy has prevailed. Analysis of all marriages in the Islands, decade by decade from 1912 to 1977, indicates a steady increase in the proportion of out-marriages among the nine recognized ethnic groups, from 11.5 percent in the first period to 38.6 percent in the last. A variety of factors, including the numerical size, ratio of men to women, and prevailing traditions toward marriage have figured prominently in the variations between groups in their rates of out-marriage. For example, the Chinese immigrants, almost wholly male, withouth their own women in the early period, had to find brides in other ethnic groups. The Japanese, on the other hand, with a fairly high proportion of women among the immigrant group, and able to secure picture brides from Japan, could adhere more readily to traditional values. The consequent widespread assumption among outsiders that the Japanese were stubbornly and implacably ethnocentric has been disproven by the out-marriage rates of 40 percent among Japanese grooms and of 47 percent among Japanese brides in the early 1980s.

The aggregate trend throughout the present century has been clearly toward greater individual freedom in the selection of marriage mates, and hence in greater mixture among the resulting progeny. Indeed the time may already have arrived when it has become impossible for many Islanders to know for certain whether they are descended from only one, two or several racial stocks. Thus two complementary trends exist in the Islands: People cling proudly and resolutely to only the one known or cherished branch of their ancestry as if it alone existed, and people find equal or greater satisfaction in the variety and richness of their dual or multiple heritage. Fortunately for Hawaii, both trends are likely to continue.

ISLAND FAUNA: OF FEATHERS AND WINGS by Alan C. Ziegler

In the cities and towns of Hawaii, common mynahs, close relatives of the kind that can learn to speak, strut boldly about on sidewalks and lawns, periodically affirming their presence by loud squawks.

Large spotted doves and their numerous smaller cousins, the zebra doves, search the ground for seeds and fruit, and may even invade the tables of open-air restaurants seeking tidbits, where they are joined by English sparrows and house finches.

If you choose to picnic in one of the many grassy parks, you can be almost sure a hungry gray-and-white red-crested cardinal or two will soon be hopping nearby, while in the shrubbery and trees the small hyperactive green birds with yellowish throats are Japanese white-eyes – or silver-eyes as Australian visitors call them. Small flocks of brownish sparrow-like birds with speckled underparts feeding on grass seeds will be nutmeg mannikins.

In larger parks and other open areas, especially on Oahu, a surprising number of escaped or intentionally released cage birds have established populations: tiny strawberry finches, Java sparrows, pin-tailed whydah finches, yellow-fronted canaries, orange-cheeked and lavender waxbills, and so on. A small group of parakeets and an occasional single larger cockatoo or macaw may even fly overhead.

As you move from urban to residential areas on Oahu, probably the first bird you will see is the blackish red-vented bulbul; even a brown-and-white red-whiskered bulbul is sometimes apparent. All-red male northern cardinals and their brownish mates, familiar to most North Americans, will be seen or heard frequently, sometimes joined by a solitary mockingbird. In extensive grassy fields, European and Japanese visitors may recognize the distinctive flight song of the skylark and, if you are from other parts of eastern Asia, you may be surprised to see such residents of your homeland as the Chinese thrush or *hwa-mei*, and the red-billed leiothrix. Or, winging overhead in Oahu's Halawa Valley, the gray swiftlet, which makes the familiar edible nests. From nearby woods will come the songs of the rust-breasted shama thrush and the obscurely colored Japanese bush-warbler or *uguisu*, although you will seldom glimpse these songsters without a search.

Large, stately, white birds in pastures or freshly cut city lots are the insect-eating cattle egrets, while substantial wraiths gliding silently over roadways at night will prove to be foraging barn owls. If you should happen to be a game-bird enthusiast, on the various main Hawaiian Islands you will find wild turkeys; ring-necked, green and kalij pheasants; chukar partridges, as well as three types of francolins; California, gambel's and Japanese quail; and mourning doves. Wild peacocks also turn up in unexpected places.

But all of these different species of birds – and another dozen or two from among the more than 150 kinds of birds introduced here – interesting and colorful as many may be, are not the real Hawaiian birds. These commonly seen town and country birds are simply hardy, adaptable species brought here from, literally, the four corners of the earth, between about 1850 and 1950, to offset the dearth of lowland native song and game birds.

It is true, at the seashore and on the coastal islets of the six main islands, as well as on the small rocky pinnacles and low sandy atolls making up the Northwestern Hawaiian Islands, you will find many kinds of birds that were not introduced by man. During most of the year on the main islands you may find three types of boobies: red-footed (some nesting on the grounds of Oahu's Sea Life Park), brown and masked; half a dozen species of small terns; storm-petrels (or »Mother Carey's chickens« of mariners); four or five larger petrels and shearwaters; red-tailed and white-tailed tropicbirds, some of the latter nesting far inland in volcanic crater walls; and the graceful great frigatebird or *'iwa,* which makes its living pirating food from hapless boobies in flight. (Occasional vagrant sea gulls of several species are seen here but, for reasons unknown, none has ever become established.)

On the Northwestern Hawaiian chain, many of these same species occur, along with the seasonally multitudinous nesting black-footed and Laysan albatrosses or »gooney birds.« On rivers and freshwater ponds of the state are found migratory ducks: primarily the mallard, northern pintail, northern shoveler, lesser scaup, American wigeon and green-winged teal. Shorebird migrants include the wandering tattler, Pacific golden-plover (with individuals setting up exclusive feeding territories on city and residential lawns during their eight-month annual sojourn in Hawaii), ruddy turnstones, sanderlings and bristle-thighed curlews. However, almost all of these birds of ocean and shore are common, widespread species – only three of which are represented by native Hawaiian subspecies – already well-known to naturalists in, at least, the countries of the Pacific world.

Where, then, are the uniquely Hawaiian birds? Where are the once-numerous black-and-yellow native honeyeaters or *'o'o* of feather cape fame, about which you may have heard or read? Where are the many species fully, even restore some ecosystems and species to a semblance of their former natural condition and abundance. Still, although the present Hawaiian native avifauna is but a shadow of its original plentitude and variety – with almost all of its 35 species of land and freshwater species officially listed as endangered – a hike with a pair of binoculars into the higher-elevation forests of most of the main islands will reveal enough of the original Hawaiian birds to allow some idea of their former splendor.

In the large 'ohia-lehua trees, numerous crimson *'apapane* forage for nectar and insects among the similarly colored blossoms. An occasional *'i'iwi*, with vermilion body, black wings and stout downcurved salmon-colored bill, may be seen there also, although it often feeds lower in the forest on the long-tubed flowers of such understory plants as native lobelias. (Both of these species are Hawaiian honeycreepers as are most of the other surviving small native songbirds, but few have been given English common names.) Greenish *'amakihi* are often as abundant as the 'apapane in the foliage of native trees, while the slightly shorter billed Hawaiian creeper, with adults of the different island races varying in color from red or brownish to yellow to green, tends to shun the tree foliage and instead utilizes the branches and trunk in its constant search for insects. These species, currently the four most abundant and widespread Hawaiian honeycreepers, can be found on most or all of the six main islands. Most of the following honeycreepers can now be seen on only one or two of the various Hawaiian Islands.

The *'akepa* has a short slightly twisted beak, possibly originally evolved for twisting open flower buds in search of insects. Its males are green and yellow on Kauai but orange on Maui and ruby red on Hawaii. Two Kauai specialties are the generally yellowish *'anianiau*, the smallest honeycreeper, and the scarce Kauai *'akialoa*, with its enormously long downcurved bill. Also found on this island (and on Maui) are the rare green-and-yellow *nuku-pu'u*, possessing a very thin tightly curled bill, and the somewhat finch-beaked greenish *'o'u* (also found on Hawaii), whose males sport an all-yellow head. Maui shelters the only living populations of the crested honeycreeper, with light-colored topknot and curiously mottled black, orange and white body; the arboreally acrobatic Maui parrot-bill; and the *po'ouli*, an enigmatic brownish black-faced species known to science only since 1973. In addition to the other honeycreepers already noted as occurring there, the Big Island of Hawaii is home of the *palila*, a finch-beaked, bean-eating species with yellow head in both sexes, now limited in range to a small area of high-mountain native forest, and the

'akiapola'au, with stout straight lower mandible for pecking or prying off tree bark, and a long, thin curved upper one for extracting insect larvae so exposed. The only honeycreepers still existing in the Northwestern Hawaiian Islands are the Nihoa and Laysan finches, now both relatively abundant and inordinately tame sparrowlike birds that survive on whatever food they can find on their tiny desolate islands: seeds, flower buds, insects and, rather amazingly, seabird eggs.

On one of these same Northwestern Islands is found the Nihoa millerbird, a native representative of the Old World warbler group. Several other small native songbirds that may be seen on the main islands represent additional founding families. The several unique Hawaiian species of the Southwest Pacific honeyeater family are now extinct or essentially so: A single individual yellow-thighed black *'o'o* is presently living out its lonely existence in the depths of Kauai's remote Alaka'i swamp, although a recent report of a similarly colored bird seen on Maui raises hope that the latter island's species may still be extant. A small rufous-and-white wrenlike bird greeting hikers along trails of Kauai, Oahu and the Big Island, often at quite low elevations, will be the *'elepaio*, closely related to certain Southwest Pacific Old World flycatchers. In the high rain forests of all main Islands except Oahu and Lanai, you may catch a glimpse of the native Hawaiian thrush, and on Kauai this species shares the Alaka'i Swamp with a still rarer bird, the small Kauai thrush.

Most of the larger native forest and freshwater birds have been mentioned previously, but note should also be made of the Hawaiian goose or *nene*, probably derived from a race of the Canada goose, and now found feeding and nesting mostly in the upland lava-flow areas of Maui and Hawaii. The Hawaiian duck, along with the Laysan duck descended from the essentially cosmopolitan mallard and colored much like the female of that ancestral species, is not uncommon on parts of Kauai, and individuals have been liberated on Oahu and the Big Island in an attempt to re-establish the species there.

This, then, has been the story of Hawaii's birds, past and present. But what about the rest of the native fauna? Some of these other animals could have been dealt with relatively easily. The only native mammals, for instance, are a race of the strong-flying North American hoary bat and a unique species of monk seal that still hauls out on the beaches of the Northwestern Hawaiian Islands. True, humpback whales from Alaskan waters journey annually to calve in the shallow waters close off Maui, much to the delight of whale watchers; and spinner porpoise and related species do cavort here year-round. But almost all of these ceta-ceans can be seen in other parts of the Pacific. (One exotic mammal on Oahu is of interest, however: the marsupial brush-tailed rock wallaby that, after escape of a single pair some 70 years ago, established a still-flourishing colony on a lava cliff here.)

No frogs, salamanders, lizards or freshwater turtles reached Hawaii, at least without the aid of man, and the only snake here is an introduced, blind earthworm-sized species. Giant green sea turtles nest on North-western Chain atolls, and several other species of these marine reptiles occasionally visit Hawaiian waters but, like the whales and porpoises, no species is restricted to the state. The few native freshwater fish and inver-tebrates, all derived from local saltwater forms, are of interest only to a few specialists – and some old-time Hawaiian fishermen. Record-size blue marlin make the west coast of the Big Island a mecca for billfishing enthusiasts but these, as well as most species of the beautiful and locally abundant reef fish and mollusks, are also widely distributed elsewhere in the Pacific world.

It is the native Hawaiian insects and similar inverte-brates, as well as the tropical tree snails, that are at least as spectacular as the Hawaiian birds, albeit on a much smaller visual scale. The dispersal of their ancestors to the Island and their subsequent evolutionary radia-tion, as well as, unfortunately, their fate, closely paral-lel those of the birds. But the many fascinating details of these lesser uniquely Hawaiian animals cannot even begin to be related here: descriptions of the preda-cious fly-catching moth caterpillars; of the myriad of pomace flies, whose 700 or more local species devel-oped from only one or two ancestors; and of the comb-footed spiders with backs painted in harlequin »happy-face« patterns. Or, of the bizarre leafhoppers whose poison-neutralizing gut is enclosed in a mas-sive unicornlike head spike; and of the damselfly nymphs that deserted ancestral streambed nurseries for rain-filled leaf bracts in trees. And, among the arboreal »singing snails,« of the profusion of shapes and colors developed by innumerable varieties in the hundreds of isolated Hawaiian mountain valleys – crea-tures so diverse that one early naturalist was moved to exclaim, fully 10 years before Darwin's theory of evolution was to appear:

»These snails never came from Noah's Ark!«

Waimea Canyon on Kauai, often called »Little Grand Canyon,« with its deep, ribboned gorges etched in greens, yellows, rusts and purples, is one of the most spectacular vistas in the Hawaiian Islands. The canyon is about 10 miles long and 2,857 feet deep at its deepest point.

Pueo is the Hawaiian name of this protected subspecies of the short-eared owl. Feeding mainly on rodents, this owl is found most often in the grasslands of all main islands. The pueo was once considered a guardian spirit of some Hawaiian families.

The Hawaiian hawk, or *'io*, was revered as a symbol of royalty in ancient Hawaiian culture. This endangered species is found only on the Big Island, where it feeds on rodents, birds and larger insects.

Hawaii's state bird, the *nene*, probably evolved from a race of the Canada goose, is found feeding and nesting in the arid upland areas of Maui and the Big Island.

French Frigate Shoals, an atoll at about the midpoint in the Hawaiian archipelago, includes the small sandy islets shown here. They provide nesting sites for sea birds and green sea turtles as well as hauling sites where Hawaiian monk seals give birth and nurse their young.

Green sea turtles bask in the sun on North Island, Pearl and Hermes Reef, part of the Hawaiian Islands National Wildlife Refuge. The female turtles lay their eggs in pits in the sand on these and other Northwestern Hawaiian Islands.

East Island, French Frigate Shoals, is a favorite basking site for seals and turtles, including this Hawaiian monk seal and her pup. The newborn pups weigh between 25 and 30 pounds and usually quadruple this weight by the time they are weaned at about 6 weeks. The monk seal is an endangered species, now probably numbering less than 1,000 animals.

Hawaii's dazzling underwater world of tropical reef fish and coral.

Whale shark, as seen from above the waters of Maui.

At the westernmost edge of Oahu is Kaena Point, accessible only by way of a rugged dirt road. Waves here sometimes reach heights of 30 and 40 feet.

Sooty terns, or 'ewa'ewa, nest by the thousands on Manana and Moku Manu islands off Oahu's windward coast and elsewhere in the Hawaiian chain.

They are one of several species of sea birds that help guide local fishermen to schools of tuna.

The largest kind of sea bird in the Hawaiian chain is the Laysan albatross, seen here at Midway in the Northwest Hawaiian Islands. Albatross begin nesting in November and their young do not depart the islands until June or July.

On Eastern Island at Midway, a great frigatebird is feeding its young. The graceful frigates nest in spring and summer. Their Hawaiian name, 'iwa (thief), refers to their habit of pirating food from boobies and other sea birds in flight.

The sea was the principal source of protein for the Hawaiians. The men primarily fished in the deep sea or along the reef from canoes; the women used hand nets along the shores to secure smaller fish, crabs and edible sea plants. Outrigger canoes, used in fishing and in canoe races, shown here on one of the black sand beaches on the Big Island. The sand was ground from lava by wave action.

A group of paddlers from the Koloa Canoe Club training off Kauai's Poipu beach for upcoming canoe races. The outrigger canoes used in races are made from either fiberglass or, in the style of the ancient Hawaiians, from wood of the majestic *koa* tree.

▷

The Hale O Keawe heiau was built in honor of Keawe-i-kckahi-aliʻi-o-ka-moku, one of the high chiefs of the Big Island of Hawaii, in 1650. It is one of three temples within Puʻuhonua O Honaunau, a Place of Refuge, a sanctuary for people who were *kapu* breakers, noncombatants or defeated warriors. The last remaining historical site of its kind, Puʻuhonua O Honaunau was restored in the 1960s and set aside as a national historic park. The annual pageant at Puʻuhonua O Honaunau opens and closes with a procession of the aliʻi and the Royal Court, including the women shown here. Also in the procession is the »birdcatcher,« an honored member of a chief's household, with his cape made from dried ti leaves.

»Auntie« Clara Ku,
a Molokai farmer,
is active in the
Hawaiian renaissance
movement.

Part of the annual
»Establishment Day
Cultural Festival« at
Pu'uhonua O Honaunau
National Historic Park
is the hula *kahiko*

(ancient), danced in
honor of the *ali'i*. The
dancers have studied
and practiced the
traditional hulas for
years.

'Iolani Palace, Hawaii's Royal Palace in Honolulu, built between 1879 and 1882, was the official residence of King Kalakaua and, later, Queen Lili'uokalani. The throne room, decorated in crimson and gold, and located on the main floor of this 140- by 100-foot building, was used for royal audiences, balls and receptions. The beautiful central staircase is fashioned from hand-carved native koa wood, as are the door and window frames. After the monarchy was overthrown in 1893, 'Iolani Palace served as the executive building for the Republic, the Territory and, finally, the state of Hawaii until the present Capitol was built. Hawaii's 19th-century monarchs incorporated European pageantry into their rule of the Islands. King Kalakaua, elected in 1874, had himself crowned in a belated coronation ceremony in 1883. Upon his death in 1891, his sister, Queen Lili'uokalani, succeeded him. She reigned for two years and was the last Hawaiian monarch.

83

The first volume of Hawaiian legends written in English was published in 1888 by Hawaii's last king, David Kalakaua. Since that time many books of folktales have been printed for youthful and adult readers. From these legends the reader may learn about both the real and the unreal in Hawaiian life – the deeds of gods, ghosts, heroes and ordinary humans. Heroes often possessed supernatural powers; some could change into animal forms and others even rose from the dead, perhaps several times. A number of legends from the mid-1800s were influenced by stories from the Bible.

CLOTHING

In the mild climate of Hawaii adults were comfortable in brief, simple garments. In most families children wore no clothing until 5 or 6 years of age. Adults bathed, swam and surfed without encumbering garments. Warriors, when engaged in hand-to-hand fighting, wore a coating of coconut oil. The feather cloaks of the chiefs were considered royal regalia, not clothing.

Men wore a loincloth, usually of bark-cloth, sometimes in the original white or dyed in solid colors or stamped with patterns of several shades. This garment, about 9 inches wide, was passed between the thighs and secured around the waist.

The woman's bark-cloth saronglike skirt extended from the waist to the knees. The material was usually decorated and long enough to pass around the body several times and be secured by tucking in the end.

For warmth, both sexes sometimes wore a rectangular bark-cloth shawl which was thrown over the shoulders.

Bark-cloth strips were pounded together while wet to form larger sheets for bedding. The tall oracle towers in the temples were covered by sheets of bark-cloth. Also, bark-cloth wisps were twisted into wicks for oil lamps and other pieces were used for bandages.

Bark-cloth, or *kapa*, was pounded from the inner bast fibers of the paper mulberry plant and from the tissues of a few other shrubs. Although the actual making of the cloth was women's work, the men used their stone adzes to hew wooden beaters and smooth logs on which to soften and flatten the plant fibers.

In addition to preparing durable clothing from the bark, the women employed a longer process of soaking, fermenting, softening and felting the fibers until they could be pounded into gauze-thin sheets of extremely fine quality. These sheets were decorated by an intricate dyeing process, then shaped into skirts for the chiefesses and into large sheets for soft bedding. Hawaiian bark-cloth is recognized as the finest in the Pacific.

PRODUCING AND SERVING FOOD

The food needed for the population, estimated at 300,000 in 1778, was produced almost entirely by the men. According to custom the men planted, harvested, cooked and served the food from the plantations. The men, who made and sailed or paddled the canoes, fished in the deep sea or along the reef for the principal supply of protein food. One of the few food-getting tasks of the women was to fish along the shores with hand nets to secure small fish, shell fish, crabs and edible sea plants. Most of these foods were eaten raw.

Plant Foods

The islands support intensive agriculture in many areas. The sunny, subtropical climate, rich soil and sufficient water encourage plant growth throughout the year. The soil is lava rock disintegrated by weathering and enriched by decayed plant materials.

Useful plants, too heavy to have reached the islands by floating or being carried by winds or birds, were brought by the early settlers in their canoes. About two dozen important plants must have been a vital part of the cargo of the colonists.

Since the planters cultivated but a few acres each, they were able to observe closely the individual plants in their gardens. They could detect genetic differences that appeared and remove the unusual plants to plots for special attention. They discovered new varieties in this way and propagated those with useful qualities.

The planter used but one tool, a sturdy planting stick 2 to 6 feet long and pointed or flattened at the ends. His strong hands and bare feet served him well in gardening.

Food plants that provided starch were taro, sweet potato, breadfruit, banana, yam and arrow root.

Of these, taro was the favorite; it grew in the rich soil of flooded ponds or in the fertile uplands where rainfall was sufficient.

The taro planters were resourceful and efficient engineers. They built countless numbers of walled ponds in the fertile soil of the valleys. They constructed canals to bring cold, fresh water from mountain springs or streams to the uppermost terraces from which it could flow down and irrigate the entire complex of ponds.

Taro and other food crops grown in upland gardens were carried down to the seaside villages in wooden or gourd bowls. These were held in nets, one suspended from each end of a sturdy carrying pole.

Religious rites, a part of all Hawaiian undertakings,

were observed with special reverence in the cultivating and processing of taro. Taro was associated with the major gods Kane and Lono and with the ancestral god Haloa.

Taro produced no viable seeds so it was propagated by planting slips which consisted of a thick slice of the top of the root and the base of the leaf stems which grew from it. Modern planters have estimated that the colonists from the south islands might have brought fewer than two dozen different varieties of taro plants to Hawaii. In the course of the several centuries to follow, the observant planters propagated mutants until some 300 varieties were being grown at the time of the arrival of the Europeans in 1778.

After about a year of growth, the mature roots of the taro were pulled from the soil. The leaves were removed, the root was washed and steamed in the ground oven. When the root was peeled it was palatable either hot or cold. But the Hawaiians much preferred to pound the root into a paste called *poi.* This process entailed the making of wooden boards on which to pound it, stone pounders and water-tight containers to store the poi while it was fermenting.

With a stone-bladed adze the men hewed slightly hollowed poi-pounding boards from close-grained wood. A board to be used by one man was about a yard in diameter. When two men pounded, one would sit at each end of a 5- or 6-foot-long board which was nearly 2 feet wide and 3 to 5 inches thick. When in use, these were placed on a clean mat in a shady spot outdoors. Knobbed poi pounders, shaped somewhat like an inverted mushroom, were usually chipped from close-grained lava rock. These might weigh as much as 7 pounds or more.

A small amount of water was added to the cooked taro as it was being pounded. The resulting thick paste was placed in a wooden or gourd bowl and covered. When needed, it was thinned with more water, allowed to ferment for two or more days and eaten.

Domestic Animals

Three land animals, the pig, dog and chicken, which the Polynesian settlers had brought with them, were used for food and as offerings in the temple. Also, certain parts of their bodies were used decoratively.

Pigs were raised in large numbers for food (for men only) and for offerings at religious ceremonies. Hawaiian historian David Malo wrote of a prayer service during which, over a period of three days, 1,840 hogs were cooked and offered in the ceremony to free a sacrificial temple from kapu. The chiefs, the priests, their attendants and the worshippers at this ceremony ate the flesh of the hogs. So necessary were these animals as temple offerings that it is unlikely that many ordinary citizens had the opportunity to taste hog meat.

Long, curved ivorylike boars' tusks, usually 19 to 24 in number, were fastened together to make a bracelet. A male dancer would wear one on each wrist.

In the early days the flesh of the dog was preferred to that of the pig. The entire family ate dog meat. Although puppies were fondled, mature dogs were not kept as pets or watchdogs.

The most spectacular articles made with dogs' teeth were the pairs of leg ornaments for the dancers. A large ornament required nearly 1,000 canine teeth. These were pierced near the root and woven securely into the mesh of the legging so closely that the teeth covered the mesh. The teeth rustled with the movements of the dancer.

Chickens foraged around the village and in the lower forest. Their flesh was bland when compared to that of the pig, dog and fish. The eggs were not eaten but left in the nests to propagate more fowls.

The roosters were prized in the popular sport of cockfighting. Cooked chickens were offered to the family gods and the temple gods.

Feathers of the cock ornamented the decorative disk of the dance gourd and some of the early designed capes of the lesser chiefs.

Fishing

A family of fishermen needed a sturdy outrigger canoe, several kinds of nets and fishlines of varying sizes made from the strong fibers of a plant endemic to Hawaii. They made their fishhooks from shell, turtle shell and animal or human bones.

Before launching the canoe, a member of the party would pause at a simple stone shrine and utter a prayer to the god of fishermen. He would vow to stop on the return and offer the first fish caught. If the fishing expedition was a village undertaking, the catch would be divided among the families represented in the venture.

In early times the chiefs supervised the building of walled shoreline fishponds, the only structures of this nature in the Pacific islands. Young fish, placed in the ponds to mature, were in most cases reserved for the chiefly owners. Most frequently stocked in the ponds were mullet and milk fish.

Once numbering more than 300, most ponds have been destroyed or filled by dredging. A half dozen or more are in use today; the ones that remain are prized as examples of Hawaiian ingenuity in providing sea food throughout the year, even when storms prevented fishing in the open ocean.

Methods of Cooking

In a culture without metal or clay the men were resourceful in devising a number of methods of cooking food. As was done throughout Polynesia, they made fire by friction using the fire plow.

The men, who were the cooks, steamed many of the vegetable and flesh foods in the ground ovens. The eating kapu required that the men's and women's food be cooked in separate ovens.

A typical oven was a hole dug into the earth about 2 feet deep and 4 to 8 feet across. A generous quantity of firewood was scattered over the bottom, and several dozen porous lava stones about the size of a fist were placed on the wood. The wood was burned to heat the stones red hot.

Green leaves, placed over the stones, insulated the raw food from the intense heat. More leaves, a clean heavy mat and a layer of soil completed the oven. After several hours the steamed food was removed.

Food was cooked wrapped in leaves or unwrapped over glowing coals. Raw meat and vegetables were placed in a heavy wooden bowl with hot stones. A lid kept the steam in and the food was cooked in a few hours.

TRANSPORTATION

People and their produce were transported from village to village or between the islands in outrigger or double canoes. On land, in this culture without wheels or beasts of burden, men walked along simple trails carrying products in containers suspended from the ends of carrying poles.

The single dugout canoe, steadied by an outrigger on its port side, was paddled or sailed along coastal waters between villages. It was capable of navigating the sometimes stormy channels between the islands. Some canoes could accommodate up to eight paddlers along with a cargo of garden produce and craft articles stored fore and aft.

Two hulls of equal or nearly equal length were secured together by cross booms, leaving 6 to 8 feet between them, to form the double canoe. A platform on the booms accommodated passengers and cargo. Large double canoes with sails had come to Hawaii from the south centuries ago bringing the first Polynesian colonists. For these long voyages a thatched structure was built on the platform between the canoes to provide shelter for the passengers and perishable cargo. The

chiefs continued to maintain large double canoes for friendly visits to neighboring islands or to transport warriors and weapons when invading other islands. Eventually these canoes were outmoded by European sailing vessels.

The canoes were hewn by stone adzes from trunks of huge endemic trees which grew in the rain forests, miles from the seaside villages. With considerable ceremony the trees were cut, partly hollowed to lighten them, then dragged to the village to be completed.

Captain Cook's officers counted over 2,500 single and double canoes that had come to greet the Englishmen and their sailing ships at Kealakekua upon their second landing in 1779.

NON-VERBAL COMMUNICATION

Women sent and received messages as they tapped their wooden beaters against the resonant logs while pounding bark-cloth.

Wooden drums with sharkskin heads were kept in a special drum house in the temple. They were brought out and the head struck with one or both hands to transmit messages by code a distance of a mile or more. Resonant lava stones, called bell stones, carried news some distance when pounded with another stone. Signal fires were known to have sent information between the islands.

Petroglyphs, symbols or figures incised in stone, are interpreted as attempts to record events or to leave messages for travelers who were expected to pass by. Hundreds of petroglyphs have been photographed and an attempt is being made to decipher their meanings.

Certain body gestures conveyed messages without the need of a word being spoken. A few of the many known gestures are: lifting the eyebrows to mean »yes«; tilting the head to indicate a direction, since one never pointed with a finger; rotating the upraised hand for »no«; hooking one's index fingers together to seal a bargain; and showing the tip of the tongue for »no« or extending the length of the tongue in defiance.

EDUCATION

Education in early Hawaii was practical and direct. From late childhood, boys and girls acquired the knowledge and skills needed to be useful citizens by learning in close association with the adults.

Young men, according to their maturity, participated in planting, fishing, constructing and sailing canoes, building houses and engaging in all activities necessary to the life of the family and the village. Boys with special talents were trained to be priests in the temples and practitioners of the healing arts.

Girls learned the art of making and dyeing bark-cloth, plaiting mats and baskets, inshore fishing and baby care.

Boys in the chiefly families were trained by selected older men in the arts of warfare, in reciting their genealogies, in their duties in the temples and court protocol.

The dance and a special type of wrestling were taught to selected students in special structures by highly skilled teachers.

This type of wrestling and body manipulation that trained bodyguards for the rulers was taught in a thatched structure. This dangerous form of hand-to-hand fighting included the secret methods of paralyzing a victim by placing pressure on certain nerves and the knowledge and skill of bone-breaking. Some say that these experts learned to pull people's arms and legs out of joint, then place them back again.

Dance and Chant

The hula and its accompanying chants were taught in a boarding school setting, also in a large, airy thatched building. Training extended over many months and discipline was rigid, but the pupils were inspired by the enthusiasm of their teachers and their respect for the patron gods and goddesses of this profession.

Upon the completion of their training, the pupils invited their parents and friends to graduation exercises during which they displayed their chanting and dancing skills.

Music, as expressed in the chant and the dance, was the most dramatic artistic outlet of the people. The chanter spoke for them as he revealed their love for the members of the family; the respect for and the awe of the forces of nature; the deeds of the gods, heroes and chiefs; and the sadness at parting. The words were more important to the listeners than the vocal forms by which they were expressed. The intoned notes of the chant were few and simple, but the words revealed meanings from the mind and heart.

Chants without rhythm were usually unaccompanied solos employing but two or three tones, and through this medium were heard prayers addressed to the gods, name chants, lengthy genealogies and dirges for departed loved ones.

Chants composed with a marked rhythm and a range of four or five tones were associated with the hula. The beat was accentuated in most dances by the use of musical instruments. These chants and dances were devoted to a wide variety of subjects.

Adolf Bastian, a German anthropologist, was the first person to publish a part of the important but little-known Hawaiian prayer chant called the *Kumulipo*. King Kalakaua gave Bastian the chant in the late 1870s. The Hawaiian and German versions of the first 11 sections, which tell of the creation of the world and its animal and plant life, were published by Bastian in Leipzig in 1881. A number of English translations with commentaries have been made since and are being studied with great interest. One of the most interesting but less known translations into English of this chant of over 2,000 lines is the one by Queen Liliuokalani who received the Hawaiian text from her brother, King Kalakaua.

The Instruments

In islands without metal or clay, the craftsmen were ingenious enough to make some 18 different kinds of musical instruments and sound-makers. Seven of these are of local invention and three are improved forms of instruments known in the islands to the south. More than half of these are used with the hula.

One or more conch shells are blown to announce the arrival of dignitaries or the beginning of a ceremony.

A chanter uses the following instruments to establish the rhythm for the hula: a coconut trunk drum with sharkskin head, a coconut shell drum with fishskin head, a large double gourd drum.

Dancers use one or two of the following instruments in their hands while dancing: a gourd rattle topped with a disk of feathers, a triple gourd rattle rotated by a pull cord, a length of bamboo with a split end that rustles, a single gourd held in one hand and struck with the other, and two stone castinets held in each hand.

A dancer might move one foot on a treadle board, keep time with a pair of rhythm sticks held one in each hand, or cause a rustle as he dances wearing dog-tooth leglets containing several hundred dogs' teeth woven into a strong netting.

Not associated with the hula were the three-string musical bow, the bamboo nose-flute and the soft-toned gourd nose whistle. Lovers used these to serenade one another at night.

SPORTS AND GAMES

In the Hawaiian calendar of events, a period of approximately four months was dedicated to the god Lono, patron of sports. The time, mid-November to mid-February in today's calendar, was least favorable for agriculture, fishing and outdoor construction. During

Japan in the early years. From 1906 Filipinos came in large numbers.

Most of the children and grandchildren of the early laborers left the plantations and came to the towns and the cities to be educated. They sought positions in the professions and with the government and founded businesses of their own. They became aggressive competition for the Hawaiians who were also seeking jobs.

☐ 1893. Queen Liliuokalani was deposed by American professional and business men thus bringing an end to the Kingdom of Hawaii. The Islands were annexed by the United States in 1898 and became a Territory in 1900. The remaining Crown lands and Hawaiian government lands were ceded to the United States. By this time individual Hawaiians owned comparatively little land in their own country.

THE REVIVAL

Yet despite the steady decline in Hawaiian ways from the time of the early contacts with foreigners, there have been a number of positive accomplishments:

☐ Hawaiian was a spoken language until expressed in writing by the missionaries who first arrived from New England in 1820. Ministers from the mission who were familiar with Latin, Greek and Hebrew sat in study sessions with Hawaiian chiefs who were experts in their own language and culture. Together they listened to the sounds and discussed the pronunciation of Hawaiian words.

It was not possible to express precisely every sound in this language of Indo-Malay origin by using letters from the English alphabet. However, by using just 12 letters, they were quite successful in accomplishing this task.

The vowels are: a, e, i, o, u. The consonants are: h, k, l, m, n, p, w. A continued study of the language through the years showed that two diacritical marks were necessary when writing certain words in order that they may be pronounced correctly and convey the proper meaning. These markings are the macron and the glottal stop.

The letters t or k, common in words from other Polynesian dialects, have been omitted frequently in Hawaii and replaced with a hamzah, or glottal stop. This mark is typed as an apostrophe and printed as a single initial quotation mark. Example: lizard might be written *moto* or *moko* elsewhere. In Hawaii, it is *mo'o*.

The macron, a short horizontal line over vowels, causes the sound to be lengthened or stressed. *Malama,* meaning »light«, is changed to »care for« by writing and pronouncing it *mālama.*

The latest dictionary, published in 1986, contains about 29,000 Hawaiian words. The extensive body of literature in Hawaiian is in the form of chants, fictional tales, historical accounts and proverbial sayings. The language is rich in words describing nature and family relationships.

☐ In the 1870s and 1880s King Kalakaua saved the existing chants and dances (banned for a half century by the missionaries) by bringing the few remaining hula masters to his court to perform and to teach others.

The king, his brother and two sisters composed numerous melodies, many of which were a blend of Hawaiian and popular music of the time. Hawaiian musicians today have continued the practice of composing songs to commemorate the many special occasions that occur throughout the year.

☐ Prince Kuhio, Hawaii's delegate to the Congress of the United States, sponsored the Hawaiian Homes Commission Act (1920–21) which set aside nearly 200,000 acres of government land for ranch, farm or residential leases for persons of one-half or more Hawaiian ancestry. More than 3,000 leases have been granted through the years but more than twice that number of persons are on the waiting list. Lack of money has prevented the commission from developing additional vacant lands for leaseholds.

Prince Kuhio also founded the Honolulu Hawaiian Civic Club to promote educational, cultural and social activities for Hawaiians and others who are interested. There are now more than 30 active clubs in Hawaii and three in California.

☐ Interest in long-distance navigation was revived in 1973–74 when members of the Polynesian Voyaging Society built the 60-foot double-hulled canoe, *Hokule'a,* and launched it at Kualoa Park, Oahu, on March 8, 1974.

Hokule'a, Star of Gladness, is the Hawaiian name for the bright star Arcturus which passes directly over Hawaii. Hoku 'A'a, Glowing Star, passes over Tahiti. It is Sirius, the Dog Star, brightest of all stars.

In 1976, *Hokule'a* set sail with a crew of 17 men and no modern navigational instruments, heading for Tahiti, 3,000 miles away. The voyage south took from May 1 to June 4; the return trip, with a crew of 11 men and two women, from July 4 to July 26.

On March 16, 1980, a trained crew sailed *Hokule'a* from Hawaii and arrived in Tahiti on April 17. The return voyage took from May 13 to June 6. Again, no modern navigational instruments were used. The principal navigator made use of his knowledge of the stars, winds, ocean swells and the flight of birds.

Encouraged by the knowledge and inspiration resulting from the canoe's round-trips to Tahiti in 1976 and

1980, the Polynesian Voyaging Society has launched and completed its ambitious, two-year, 13,000-mile Voyage of Rediscovery. In July 1985, the *Hokule'a,* with its skilled navigator Nainoa Thompson and its trained crew of about a dozen men and women, sailed from Hawaii to Tahiti; in September to the Cook Islands and in December to New Zealand. After an extended period of waiting for proper weather conditions, the journey continued to Tonga in May 1986; later that month to Samoa and in July back to the Cook Islands. From there, the voyage continued to Tahiti. And in April 1987 to the Tuamotus Islands, and from there back to Hawaii, where the canoe and its crew arrived in May 1987.

At each stop the crew members visited with the resident islanders and confirmed their pride in the rich Polynesian culture which they shared. The Voyage of Rediscovery became a Voyage of Inspiration.

□ Two organizations that are now exerting great influence for the betterment of the Hawaiian people are the Office of Hawaiian Affairs (OHA) and Alu Like.

The Office of Hawaiian Affairs is a state agency provided for by the revised state constitution of 1980. It coordinates services and programs for Hawaiians living in Hawaii through a board of nine trustees. The latest board was elected by 43,064 voters of Hawaiian ancestry in the 1984 elections.

Funds for OHA's operating expenses are derived from the Public Land Trust Fund, about a million and a half dollars a year, and from the state Legislature, which authorizes about a half-million dollars a year.

Alu Like (»Working Together«) is a private, non-profit organization devoted to achieving the economic and social self-sufficiency of the Hawaiian people. It was formed in 1974 when the Congress of the United States made Hawaiians eligible for funds from the office of the Indian and Native American Program. As much as $ 7 million in Alu Like's annual budget comes from these federal funds.

Many of the Hawaiian people today are struggling to cope with such problems as lack of land, a feeling of inferiority resulting from the loss of identity and culture, the unfavorable impact of tourism, business competition from the overwhelming number of non-Hawaiians (Hawaiians own less than 3 percent of Island businesses), the lowest median family income in the state and a high incidence of disease.

Despite these serious problems, many Hawaiian people are now actively involved in a renaissance, a renewal of many phases of their culture. This spirit of rebirth is evident economically, artistically, politically and socially. The movement is not only reviving and preserving the traditional, but is forging ahead to promote the economic and cultural welfare of the people. A number of non-ethnic Hawaiians are also participating and promoting phases of the renaissance in their areas of expertise.

The renaissance is reversing the cultural decline and providing a psychological renewal that is bringing to some of the participants, for the first time in their lives, pride in being Hawaiian. Among the happenings are:

A group of Hawaiian artists has organized and is showing its work regularly in local galleries.

Musicians of Hawaiian ancestry are playing in many of the nightclubs in Waikiki and other visitor areas. About 20 years ago there was only one Hawaiian show for the tourists.

More hula studios are training a larger number of young men and women than ever before. Hula festivals are attended by thousands of spectators.

The native pastime of surfing, once a dying sport, is practiced professionally here by surfers who come from around the world.

More than 60 outrigger canoe clubs are practicing and competing regularly. The 1976 and 1980 sailings of the canoe *Hokule'a* from Hawaii to Tahiti and back were great boosts to Polynesian pride, as is the 1985–1987 Voyage of Rediscovery.

The state constitution provides for the teaching of Hawaiian history, culture and language in the public schools. Many adults are taking these courses in night schools.

Many people are practicing the Hawaiian craft of making leis and other ornaments from feathers. Others are plaiting leaves into mats and twisting fibers into cordage.

The renaissance of the 1970s and the 1980s is the most significant movement for the Hawaiian people during this century.

Imua a lanakila – Forward to full accomplishment!

TALES OF HAWAII: THE DARING AND THE DETERMINED by Bob Krauss

As Hawaii emerged into the modern world, the least likely candidate for headlines was a quiet, unassuming Hawaiian cowboy named Koolau. Yet he fought a private war against the march of progress and became a folk hero. He did this not in bustling Honolulu but in a remote, jungle-robed valley on the cliff-bound northwest coast of the island of Kauai, an area where civilization had barely penetrated. The year was 1893. The last of the Hawaiian monarchs, Queen Liliuokalani, had just lost her throne to a consortium of white merchants and sugar planters more interested in foreign trade than Hawaiian independence.

It was not foreign trade, however, but foreign disease that had turned Koolau into a fugitive and had driven him down the cliff trail into Kalalau Valley, where some 90 Hawaiians still subsisted off the land and the sea as their ancestors had done. Four years before, Koolau had noticed lumps on his face. His skin had thickened. In time, the symptoms became too obvious to escape notice. Koolau had leprosy.

His flight into the lonely valley with Piilani, his pretty wife, and Kaleimanu, their 10-year-old son, placed him outside the law because police sternly enforced Health Department regulations requiring lepers to be sent to an isolated colony on the island of Molokai. Father Damien, the heroic Catholic priest, had died there in 1889, a victim of the disease himself. The leper colony on Molokai was known as the land of no return. Yet, Koolau would have gone there had Deputy Sheriff Louis H. Stolz permitted him to take Piilani and Kaleimanu with him. When Stolz refused, because the regulations would not allow it, Koolau had fled with his family down the precarious cliff trail.

There he joined a band of some 20 leprous refugees who lived apart in vast Kalalau Valley, an amphitheater 4 miles long and several miles wide. Water cascaded from the soaring cliffs and flowed to the sea in abundant streams. Generations ago these streams had been cleverly diverted to irrigate taro terraces built at the foot of the cliffs. There was abundant shrimp in the streams and fish in the ocean. Wild goats and pigs abounded in the heavily forested upper valley where the lepers lived. The valley produced bananas and mangoes and guavas and breadfruit.

Hawaiian residents of the valley did not fear the lepers, who were themselves Hawaiian. Here Koolau built a home for his family, planted taro and hunted for wild game. His reputation as a crack shot and expert woodsman quickly spread. He spent one of the happiest years of his life in Kalalau Valley.

But in May 1893, Kauai Deputy Sheriff Stolz decided it was time to round up the lepers. He deputized several Kauai residents and marched along an 11-mile-long coastal trail into the valley. Using tact and diplomacy he soon had a number of the fugitives in hand. But Koolau would not be cajoled. There are a number of versions of what happened. They all end the same. There was a confrontation and Stolz was left dead, one bullet in his stomach and another in his heart.

Panic spread in the valley, but it was nothing like the hysteria that gripped Honolulu after one of the deputized Hawaiians brought the grim report out of Kalalau Valley. On June 30, headlines in the *Daily Pacific Commercial Advertiser* shouted the news of Stolz's murder at the hands of outlaw lepers prepared to shoot anybody who tried to take them. The *Daily Bulletin,* however, defended the lepers in an editorial which read, »Kalalau is an ideal home for those unfortunates, being much more eligible than the Molokai corral . . .« But the president of the new revolutionary republic, Sanford B. Dole, declared a state of martial law on the entire island of Kauai and dispatched a force of militia and police – 35 fully armed officers and men – to take the dangerous lepers, dead or alive. This comic opera army set sail equipped with a Krupp howitzer, presumably for blasting the rebels from their mountain lairs.

What they found was a pitiful band of sick people in no condition to fight, even if they had wanted too. Within two days, all were in custody except for Koolau, his wife and son. The three had disappeared into the jungle at the head of the valley. On a sunny Fourth of July, the militia unlimbered its howitzer and shelled the area, then made a full-scale foray to round up Koolau. A squad of men crawled up a razorback ridge to investigate what appeared to be a barricaded hideout up in the cliff.

They found more than they had bargained for. As the squad approached the barricade, shots rang out. The lead man, hit in the chest, rolled off the ridge into a ravine below. The other members of the squad panicked and stumbled into each other. Two of them plunged into the ravine, but fortunately, escaped with only cuts and bruises.

It was Koolau, of course, who had fired from the barricade. He waited until the squad retreated, then climbed down to do what he could for the soldier he had shot. The man was still alive. Koolau made a compress of ti leaf to stop the bleeding. It did not help. The man died. Before returning to the barricade,

Koolau placed his cap under the dead man's head and folded his arms over his chest.

The expeditionary force made another charge early the next morning. When they came into range, Koolau picked off the first militiaman with a shot to the head. Again the others panicked. Koolau could have killed more, but he didn't have to. One of the soldiers shot himself in the throat in his haste to escape. By this time, the expedition commander had had his bellyful of fighting Koolau. He sent out for Koolau's sister and forced her to climb the ridge to the barricade. All she found were some cigarette butts, a few articles of clothing and part of a dried eel on which the fugitives had fed.

Koolau had quietly moved to another hiding place during the night. The militia returned to Honolulu without ever setting eyes on him. He and Piilani, with their son, made camp near a waterfall which fed nearby taro patches and banana trees. Here they lived in complete isolation, away from even the Hawaiian residents of Kalalau Valley. Before too long, the boy, Kaleimanu, died of leprosy, then Koolau himself. They are buried in the valley. Piilani, who never contracted the disease, hiked out of the valley and returned to her family. Years later, a member of the militia wrote of the futile attempt to capture Koolau, »It's a beautiful valley and the lepers should have been left in peace where they bothered no one.«

In 1898, the United States annexed Hawaii. As a result, the Islands enjoyed a modest boom in tourism and began to experience the blessings of American business enterprise. The most visible symptom of this influx of people and money was advertising. Within 10 years, the streets of Honolulu were plastered with billboards. Thus began another sequence of events that has become part of the folklore of modern Hawaii.

The billboards popped up all over town. A huge sign advertising soap adorned historic Punchbowl Crater. In lush Manoa Valley, where there had been tropical foliage, there now blossomed enormous billboards advertising chewing gum. One billboard proclaimed: BOWLERS NEVER GET APPENDICITIS – TRY BOWLING FOR STOMACH FAG. Tourists enroute to Waikiki saw not only picturesque coconut palms but enormous signs advertising whiskey and hair lotion and Bull Durham tobacco and toilet bowl cleanser.

Most merchants and other males familiar with economic development understood the virtues of these signs. Many of their wives did not. Then in 1912 a Honolulu organization for women called the Outdoor Circle provided an outlet for the growing annoyance over proliferating billboards. These women were dedicated to the beautification of Honolulu: to the planting of shade trees, removal of old fences, opening of park spaces, establishment of playgrounds for children. All these objectives were acceptable to the male business leaders of Honolulu.

But when the ladies declared war on billboards, quite a number of men felt the women should stay at home and tend to their knitting. Billboards were, after all, big business. But the ladies refused to shut up. They wrote letters to the editor. They distributed rubber stamps to members of the Outdoor Circle who then stamped all correspondence, and especially the bills they paid to local merchants, with prominent criticism of billboards. It turned out that the ladies of the Outdoor Circle also possessed an extremely effective secret weapon: They were married to some of the most powerful businessmen in town. The women waged war over the breakfast table so effectively that male solidarity was breached.

The first major break in the ranks came when Lorrin A. Thurston, publisher of the *Pacific Commercial Advertiser,* turned over one issue of his newspaper entirely to the Outdoor Circle. On May 10, 1913, the Circle produced an anti-billboard edition filled with photos of the ugliest billboards in town, anti-billboard essays by students, and laudatory stories about advertisers who had already seen the light and taken down their signs.

By this time, a few of the merchants were in full retreat. E. O. Hall & Son Ltd., hardware dealers, vowed to never again use Sherman-Williams paints to paint billboards. In all, 49 merchants took the pledge to abstain from the use of billboards. This infuriated males who were made of sterner stuff, especially those who owned billboard companies. One reader objected strenuously to an *Advertiser* editorial which listed billboards as a »necessary evil« along with saloons and houses of prostitution. Charles R. Ray, of the Pioneer Advertising Company, tried another tack. »The billboard often hides an ugly spot in the city,« he wrote diplomatically. »In spite of the attacks made upon outdoor advertising, the fact remains that many citizens prefer to see billboards to the rubbish heaps constantly despoiling vacant lots here.«

Members of the Outdoor Circle were not to be put off by such self-serving balderdash. They continued their campaign with personal calls upon owners and managers of local business firms who used billboard advertising.

As the years passed, critics who had objected to female meddling began to speak of the Outdoor Circle with respect. The ladies themselves carefully avoided the temptation to exact revenge. For example, one advertising company had gone into business before the anti-billboard campaign started, so the Circle decided it would not be fair to punish its owner for his bad business judgment. Therefore, the ladies looked up his tax returns and offered him $ 2,500 for the business, a sum they considered fair according to what he was making on his investment. He countered with a price of $ 18,000 and the deal fell through.

But the power of the Outdoor Circle increased. The members wrote letters to Mainland companies who used billboard advertising in Hawaii. At first these companies paid little attention to the protests, but then one of them papered Honolulu with advertisements for baking powder. To the consternation of company officials, not only were they deluged with angry letters but baking powder sales in Hawaii plummeted as a result of a boycott by this organization called the Outdoor Circle. The signs came down.

After that, even giant companies capitulated. In 1923, the president of Consolidated Amusement theater chain in Honolulu announced that his company was ending the use of outdoor advertising. Consolidated had been the last major holdout locally.

In 1927, the local billboard company sold all of its assets to the Outdoor Circle for $ 4,000. Outdoor Circle members had raised the money through balls and bake sales and bazaars. They immediately dismantled the company and sold the lumber used in the signs to a construction firm. In 1930, the two biggest tobacco companies in the world – American Tobacco and Liggett & Myers – pledged their cooperation in eliminating outdoor signs in Hawaii. There have not been billboards in the Islands since.

During this time, modern technology had produced a new machine for over-ocean travel, the airplane. This spawned another generation of heroes who enliven the pages of Hawaiian folklore. Among the most engaging of these daredevils was a young chap named Charles Fern.

Fern quit the University of California in his junior year to enlist in the U.S. Army Air Service during World War I. Short, stocky and brisk, Fern turned to barnstorming after the war but found that flying was no longer a novelty on the West Coast of the U.S. This daredevil needed an audience.

So Charlie and his financial partner, Ben Stoddard, decided to ship their JN4D »Jenny« two-seater biplane to Honolulu, a place where few people had ever flown in an airplane. The authorities gave them permission to use Kapiolani Park, adjacent to Waikiki, as their landing strip. By January 1920 Charlie was gainfully employed giving thrill-seeking Honolulans rides at $ 10 for 10 minutes, $ 100 for a flight around the island. For $ 25 extra, he threw in a few loop the loops and fancy turns. It was at this time that he made local aviation history by piloting the first inter-island passenger flight in Hawaii.

According to Charlie, this historic event took place because a Norwegian shipping tycoon asked Charlie if he could fly him to Maui, an island some 100 miles to the southeast of Honolulu and Oahu. Charlie replied, »Sure, where's Maui?« The Norwegian wished to visit one of the Baldwins, a Maui sugar baron, but did not have time to make the two-day voyage by sea. Charlie agreed to take him by air for $ 150 round trip. That night, at a *luau* (Hawaiian feast), a friend drew Charlie a map of Maui on the back of an envelope and indicated the location of Baldwin's polo field, a spot where an airplane could land.

The flight began early the next morning. Charlie piloted his single-engine plane over the channel to Molokai where he took special note of the cattle pastures at the Cooke ranch because they would make excellent emergency landing fields, just in case. Then the plane flew out over the ocean again toward Maui. Just then, Charlie noticed his gas gauge plummet from three-quarters full to empty. Apparently, all the gas had leaked out of his tank. He stood up in the cockpit but was unable to see any gas running out. The engine was still humming. So Charlie turned back to Molokai and landed without incident on one of the pastures he had spotted.

A check of the 20-gallon fuel tank showed that it was three-quarters full. The float of the gas gauge had sprung a leak and sunk. Charlie took off again and flew on to Maui. Once there, he could not find the polo field because it had been marked incorrectly on that envelope map. Finally he landed on the racetrack of the Maui Fair Grounds. His passenger motored to the Baldwins' while Charlie tried to solve a new problem, one unique to air transportation.

It had rained the night before and the fair grounds field was a sea of mud. Charlie had landed in the only dry spot. There was not enough dry ground, however, to take off again. Fortunately, an old college chum happened to be working on a Maui sugar plantation and with his help, Charlie rounded up a bunch of husky men the next day. He gave them instructions to hang onto the wings and struts while he opened the throttle. This would bring the tail up into flying position. When Charlie raised his arm, the men were to let go together. If they didn't let go at the exact same moment, the plane would slue around and do a ground loop. They positioned the plane and everybody grabbed hold. Charlie gave all eight cylinders full throttle and raised his arm. Fortunately, everybody let go together. Charlie said the plane nearly shot out from under him. He took off with dry ground to spare, sailed over the fair grounds fence and headed for the polo field. He picked up his passenger and an hour and 20 minutes later, they landed back at Kapiolani Park in Honolulu.

Despite this heroic demonstration of the feasibility of air transport in Hawaii, few local residents showed an interest in flying from island to island. Charlie eventually gave up flying to become editor of the weekly newspaper on Kauai. He has since retired. Charles Lindbergh's historic crossing of the Atlantic in May 1927 renewed interest in over-ocean travel. In the same year pineapple king James Dole sponsored a highly publicized air race from San Francisco to Hawaii. The event was called the Dole Derby. It turned out to be a fiasco. Of the eight planes entered, only four got into the air. Two of these made it to Hawaii. The others were never heard from again. A dozen people lost their lives in the Dole Derby.

Nevertheless, Stanley Kennedy, an enthusiastic young passenger agent for the Inter-Island Steam Navigation Company, persuaded his board of directors to inaugurate Hawaii's first airline. In 1929 the company purchased a fleet of Sikorsky flying boats. The venture was an immediate success because it overcame the biggest single deterrent to surface travel between islands: seasickness.

Kennedy's brilliant grasp of airline economics ensured the company's profitability. For example, when Inter-Island Airways opened service, the premier flight was to Kailua on the Kona Coast of Hawaii, 200 miles away. Naturally, the directors of the company were invited on this inaugural. There were eight seats on a Sikorsky flying boat and eight directors. According to Hawaii's aviation folklore, young Kennedy longed to make the trip, so the chief pilot suggested, »Why don't you sit on the toilet?« He did. For the return to Honolulu, Kennedy had the toilet taken out and a seat for a paying passenger substituted. From then on, the Sikorsky flying boats carried nine passengers instead of eight, and passengers made sure they went to the bathroom before taking off. That extra seat was one reason the airline made money.

The elite sport of polo, rich in Island folklore, provides an interesting reflection of Hawaii's social structure into the 1940s. Only the wealthy could afford to breed and train polo ponies. Lesser mortals curried them and shoveled the manure. Yet the sport has never been for sissies. It requires skill and stamina and horse sense. For decades a special aura surrounded Hawaii's championship polo players.

Even their names breathed affluence and power. On Maui it was the Baldwins, descendants of a medical missionary and heirs to a sugar dynasty. They played polo as a family. The Maui team consisted of Edward, Richard and Lawrence Baldwin, and Harold »Oskie« Rice, whose mother was a Baldwin. Edward Baldwin was considered the best polo player Hawaii ever produced. On Oahu, polo was synonymous with the Dillinghams: business tycoon Walter F. Dillingham and his sons, Gay, Lowell and Ben, heirs to an empire that began with a hardware store and grew into railroads, construction, development and shipping.

While their wealth set them apart, the Baldwins, the Dillinghams and the rest did not flaunt it. The islands were too small for that. They were generous and kind without ostentation. Of course, they went to Ivy League schools and married only their own kind. But they mingled socially with lesser humans and called them by their first names. Polo games provided an excellent opportunity for such democratic association. Anybody could drive to Kapiolani Park in a flivver and watch the nabobs at their sport.

Polo reached its zenith, as did the *haole* (white) elite of Hawaii, in the 1930s. The tournament of 1935 is considered the most exciting. Four teams were entered, including the Baldwins from Maui and the Dillinghams from Oahu, of course. The Army fielded a team led by Lt. Col. George S. Patton, who later led U.S. troops in Europe during World War II. The team to beat came from Midwick Country Club in Southern California. It was anchored by Eric Pedley, a renowned player who boasted an international reputation. Hal Roach, the movie producer, also played for Midwick.

Army took the field against the Baldwins; Patton called them the »Maui Cowboys,« a term he did not intend to be complimentary. Maui won 8–5 despite Patton's reckless, slashing style. Then Maui beat Oahu 7–6. That left only the awesome Midwick team. The largest crowd in the history of Island polo gathered at Kapiolani Park on a Sunday in August 1935 to watch the contest.

Midwick had breezed through its earlier matches. But the Maui Cowboys refused to be intimidated. They battled to a 3–3 tie at halftime. When play resumed, Maui never led but kept the score tied. The crowd was on its feet cheering in a frenzy of excitement as regulation time ended in a 5–5 tie. Whichever team scored first during the playoff would win. Lawrence Baldwin put in the winning goal. The crowd pulled the Maui Cowboys off their horses and carried them from the field.

Although Patton did not win, he left his mark on Hawaii's polo folklore. He and his Army team lost to the Baldwins the following year on their Maui polo field. That night, during a party at the Baldwin's Ulupalakua Ranch, the future general stood on his head in a doorway, braced his feet against the sides and drank down a glass filled with scotch, bourbon and gin.

The shock waves caused by Japanese bombs falling on Pearl Harbor on December 7, 1941, did more than destroy a fleet of battle-ships. They ended a way of life in Hawaii, a way of life symbolized by polo. World War II and the changes it brought ushered a whole new cast of characters into the folklore of Hawaii. Many are Oriental, sons and daughters of parents who served the haole elite. None exemplifies the new order better than an energetic, cigar-smoking, chunky Chinese named Chinn Ho. His grandfather grew taro in Waikiki. Chinn himself attended a two-room school across Kalakaua Avenue from the old Moana Hotel, a resort for haoles he was never permitted to enter.

Chinn did not go to the polo games. He played piccolo in the McKinley High School band because a piccolo was the cheapest instrument he could buy. And he saved the money for it himself. After graduation, the principal asked if he could help raise $ 38 to replace a window his classmates had broken. Chinn gathered his friends and organized a *hui*, a word meaning syndicate, and had a new window put in. He invested the money left over. Within five years his equity was worth $ 5,000.

His first job was in a bank, but he was not permitted in a teller's cage because bank policy did not allow Orientals to represent the bank to the public. A year later he went to work as a salesman for a brokerage firm. He came to work at 4:30 a. m. because at that early hour in Hawaii the New York Stock Exchange was still in operation 5,000 miles away. He could still get in on the day's trading. Other local stockbrokers could only take orders for the next day because the exchange was closed when they came to work.

Chinn Ho was never afraid to take a risk. He speculated in rubber and made about $ 7,000. Fast-stepping financial footwork kept him so busy he didn't have time to marry until he was 30. Then he proposed to a beautiful young secretary, Betty Ching. They moved into a house in Waikiki, one of three cottages for which he paid $ 5,500 with 10 percent down and monthly mortgage payments of $ 75. He collected $ 75 per month rent from each of the other two cottages and lived in the third free. Eventually he made about $ 22,000 on the deal.

When World War II came along, many property owners moved away in fear of a Japanese invasion. Chinn organized huis to buy these properties, fixed them up and sold them at a good profit. By the time the war ended he had formed his own company, Capital Investment, and was ready to take on the haole business establishment.

His baptism of fire came when he learned of a land lease that had expired in the sugar plantation town of Waipahu, not far from Honolulu. The property was small but it cut across the road used by plantation trucks to haul cane to the mill. The plantation owners had allowed the lease to expire because renegotiation had been little more than a formality in the past. This time they discovered that a Chinese investor named Chinn Ho had snapped up the lease and was now asking for a ridiculous increase in land rent. Yet they had no alternative but to pay his price. If they didn't, he could close the road and shut off access to the mill. Building a new road would cost much more than paying the new lease rent.

At this time, Chinn was capitalized for $ 150,000 in stock, had three employees and a shortwave radio set to monitor New York market quotations. His big chance came in 1947 when a friend at the Honolulu Stock Exchange asked why he wasn't bidding on Waianae Plantation. Chinn said he didn't know it was up for sale. But he knew that the land, a vast holding on the leeward side of the island, had tremendous potential because such sizable parcels seldom came on the market in Hawaii. He obtained a prospectus, then hired an engineer friend to quietly go to Waianae and make a survey. The big question was water. All this happened on a Friday. On Sunday the engineer reported back that there was water enough for development.

Chinn immediately arranged for an early Monday meeting with the president of American Factors, one of Honolulu's major firms and the owner of the land. He was there promptly at 9 a. m. with pointed questions. Was the land for sale? Yes. What was the price? A million and a quarter. Was $ 100,000 enough for a down payment? Yes. Chinn went down the street to his bank and returned with a cashier's check. The president of American Factors, taken aback, protested that Chinn hadn't proven his ability to pay the rest. Chinn said he would see to that right away.

Back on the street, he ran into the president of the bank that held mortgages on the Waianae land. Chinn explained that he could raise more than $ 750,000 in cash and spin off part of the plantation land for additional money if the bank would grant him a $ 750,000 mortgage. The bank president, eager to get his money out of Waianae, said that could be arranged. Would he so notify American Factors? He would.

By this time it was Monday noon and a dazed board of directors at American Factors had hastily met to consider Chinn Ho's offer. There was no question he had fulfilled the financial requirements. But some of the members balked at selling outside the establishment. At 1:30 p.m., they called Ho in. They wanted to know about the crop of sugar now on the land. Chinn promised them 18 months to harvest it because his engineering surveys would take that long. How about the cattle? Chinn promised them time to sell, or he would buy the cattle himself. And the plantation employees? Chinn said they could remain six months rent free. The directors had no alternative but to close the deal.

It was the first major land acquisition by an Oriental in Hawaii and it made headlines. It also launched the legend of Chinn Ho, later the model for James Michener's character Hong Kong Kee in his novel *Hawaii*, published in 1959, the year the Islands became a state. Chinn Ho went on to become the first Oriental ever elected president of the Honolulu Stock Exchange, the first to win a directorship of an establishment company and the first to become chairman of the board of a major Honolulu newspaper. The boy who was not permitted into the Moana Hotel grew up to own not only his own hotels but entire resorts as well. His latest development is the Great Wall Hotel in Peking, China.

Statehood for Hawaii and the advent of jet air travel have transformed Waikiki from the sleepy, seaside settlement Chinn Ho knew as a boy to an exciting destination resort and entertainment center. Similar changes have taken place on other islands. But folklore lives on. A typical example is the Kona Village on the Big Island's peaceful leeward coast. The Kona Village is the epitome of escape, a cluster of thatched cottages in an oasis of green, on a lava flow beside a magnificently lonely beach. There is a swimming pool, a picturesque bar and dinner by candlelight. Here there are no telephones and no crises, only endless hours of luxurious, pampered solitude. It is also very expensive, with an exclusive clientele of discriminating and wealthy visitors.

It was not easy to achieve such perfection on a remote desert of raw lava. There was no road over which trucks could bring building materials, so the contractor bought a surplus World War II landing craft at a junk yard, loaded it with lumber and concrete, sailed to the building site and ran up on the beach as if he were filming an invasion scene for a war movie. The flatbed trucks that hauled in the tile, marble tabletops and furniture had to be towed back up the lava slope. Planting palm trees turned out to be a major effort.

Holes had to be blasted in the lava down to the water level and then filled with soil. Both the palms and soil were brought in. To make things easier, the developer carved an airstrip out of the lava. Liquor and draft beer arrived by plane. So did the hotel piano.

But in the early days hotel employees came to work over the lava in a secondhand school bus – that is, if a tire didn't blow out on the way, or if the bus didn't run out of gas or water. The hotel gardener threatened to quit because a pet donkey ate up the young palm trees. Then a waitress got pregnant. And a macaw, the hotel mascot, flew into a kiawe tree and refused to come down; a bartender had to climb up through the thorns and saw off the branch.

All this has changed, of course. Airplanes now buzz in and out of the enlarged landing strip like mosquitoes. A smooth, paved road leads over the lava flow from the highway to the resort. There is an air of sophistication about the place now in keeping with Hawaii's new image. Yet people still remember those early days with the landing craft, the school bus and the donkey.

In the old days, when first-class travel meant elegant, steam-belching ocean liners, the Aloha Tower was Honolulu Harbor's most famous landmark. On »boat days« the tower was the scene of swaying hips on gracious, olive-skinned girls handing out flower leis to pale-faced *haoles* (foreigners). Today, the hula girls and the music are gone, but modern cruising ships still arrive here, and the 10th floor of the tower still offers a panoramic view of the harbor and the city.

The State Capitol of Hawaii, completed in 1969, is a bright, massive structure whose cantilevered concrete ribs are combined by glass mosaic tiles. Most of its interior is paneled in koa wood.

Bishop Street runs from the waterfront at Aloha Tower through the heart of the downtown Honolulu business district.

103

Carved out of barren lava flows at the edge of the sea on the Big Island's sunny Kohala coast, the Mauna Lani Resort's 18-hole golf course is considered one of the most beautiful in the world.

The elite sport of polo, requiring skill, stamina and horse sense, reached its zenith in Hawaii in the 1930s. For decades, a special aura surrounded Hawaii's championship polo players, including the Baldwins of Maui and the Dillinghams of Oahu. Today, teams from many countries come to compete at the Mokuleia polo grounds on the northwest shore of Oahu. Mauna Lani Resort's exclusive terrace condominiums, fishponds and Mauna Lani Bay Hotel.

The Polynesian Cultural Center on Oahu's north shore is one of the major touristic attractions in Hawaii. The center features cultural displays and villages from throughout Polynesia.

Hula dancers of modern (*'auana*) style with red dyed feather gourds at a Christmas show at the Honolulu zoo.

One of the many beautiful floral floats in the Aloha Week Parade, an annual event held every September on Oahu.

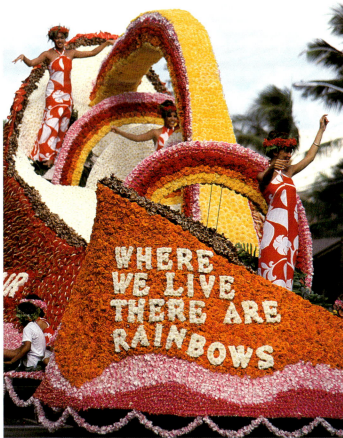

WHERE WE LIVE THERE ARE RAINBOWS

Evening entertainment in Honolulu: elegant dining at the »Pink Lady,« the Royal Hawaiian Hotel at Waikiki beach, built in 1927; exotic food and drinks on the *Oceania*, a floating Chinese restaurant brought to Honolulu from Hong Kong in 1972 (and presently out of business); dancing fun at Rumours disco in the Ala Moana Hotel.

Honolulu city lights –
Waikiki photographed
from the Sheraton-
Waikiki hotel.

▷

The USS Arizona Memorial, on the surface above the sunken battleship, honors the 1,102 crew men who were killed during the Japanese attack on Pearl Harbor on December 7, 1941. The men remain entombed in the sunken vessel. U.S. Marines reading the names of the »gallant men« who went down with the *Arizona*.

Within an extinct volcanic cone in Honolulu, which the Hawaiians called Puu-o-waina, the hill of sacrifice, is the National Memorial Cemetery of the Pacific. Now called Punchbowl, it is the burying place for the U.S. war dead of the Pacific, a solemn place of remembrance for many American families.

The sea cliffs of the northeast coast of Molokai are renowned for their rugged beauty and isolation. They are listed in the Guinness Book of World Records as the highest sea cliffs in elevation (up to 3,250 feet). Glider rides from Dillingham airfield in 3-seat sailplanes high above the wind-swept shores near Mokuleia on Oahu. Hang gliding from Makapuu cliffs on Oahu's windward side is a thrilling but dangerous challenge.

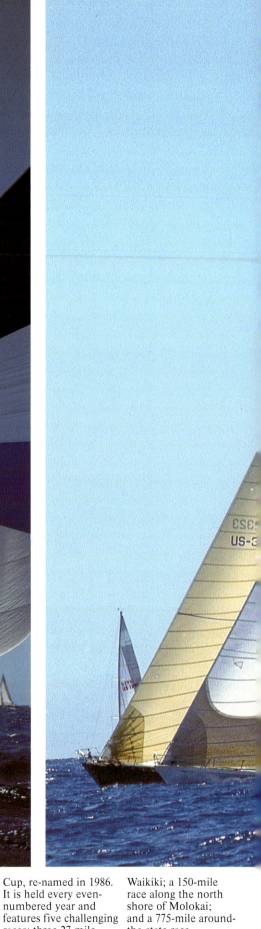

With warm waters, strong trade winds and a season that runs from January to December, Hawaii offers sailboat racing nearly every weekend.

One of the Islands' most famous races, the 2,225-nautical-mile Transpacific Yacht Race from San Pedro, California, to Honolulu is a biennial event that originated in 1906, the oldest major distance yacht race in the world.

The newest yachting event, the Kenwood Cup Hawaii International Ocean Racing Series, was inaugurated in 1978 as the Pan Am Clipper Cup, re-named in 1986. It is held every even-numbered year and features five challenging races: three 27-mile Olympic triangles off Waikiki; a 150-mile race along the north shore of Molokai; and a 775-mile around-the-state race.

The Hawaiian Ironman Triathlon World Championship in and around Kailua-Kona on the Big Island every October is considered the Super Bowl of races. This ultra-endurance event starts with a 2.4-mile roughwater swim, is followed by a 112-mile bicycle ride and ends with a 26.2-mile marathon run, all done on the same day. Winner of the triathlon shown here is Dave Scott.

Michael Ho of Oahu, considered one of the world's finest big-wave riders, here rides the »right« break at Banzai Pipeline on Oahu's north shore. The quickly breaking tubes look like a pipeline and give the beach its name.

In Hawaii the fishing season is year round, although the best months are May through November. Big game fish caught here include *a'u* (Pacific blue marlin), *mahimahi* (dolphin fish), *ahi* (yellowfin tuna), *aku* (tuna), *ulua* (jack) and *ono* (wahoo).

During the August 1986 Hawaiian International Billfish Tournament, one of the oldest amateur fishing competitions in the Pacific, Gil Kraemer of California caught this record 1,062$\frac{1}{2}$-pound marlin.

Artificial lures, made by experienced anglers to attract the big game fish of Hawaii's waters, are as colorful as a Las Vegas showgirl.

123

HAWAII OUTDOORS: YEAR-ROUND FUN AND FITNESS by Carol Hogan

 awaii is famous for its white sand beaches and warm tropical waters. The image is one of sun-baked relaxation. That's why most visitors are surprised to learn what residents already know: The Hawaiian Islands offer a dazzling array of recreational pursuits – including some that require ice and snow.

There is never a day that you can't enjoy Hawaii outdoors. Let's examine these sports and games, beginning with ocean activities, naturally the most popular pastime in a state surrounded entirely by water.

Hawaiian *outrigger canoe paddling* remains one of the last Hawaiian sports taken seriously in the Islands. For many paddlers, love of the sport begins with interscholastic league competition and continues into adulthood as a family activity.

Canoe clubs from all islands compete according to rules designated by the Hawaiian Canoe Racing Association (HCRA). Interclub races are held almost every weekend, starting with an unofficial double-canoe event in late May. The official season opens with Oahu's Kamehameha Day Regatta in June. Short-distance, closed-course races occur every weekend until the State Championships in August.

Long-distance competition begins after that, culminating in the women's Na Wahine O Ke Kai in September and the men's Molokai Hoe in October. Both races are 40.8 miles, from Molokai to Oahu, across the Kaiwi Channel.

The Kaiwi Channel is one of the world's roughest stretches of water, often rolling with huge swells and buffeted by strong winds. Crossing it in a six-person canoe was originally considered a feat for men only. The men first crossed it in 1952.

Then, to prove it could be done, women from Healani and Onipaa canoe clubs paddled across in 1975. Four years later 17 women's teams completed the inaugural Na Wahine race and it is now an annual event.

Some people prefer racing one-person *kayaks* and *surfskis*. The Kanaka Ikaika kayak club and the Hawaii Kayak Racing Association organize races of increasing distances from November until May, when the Kanaka Ikaika 29-mile race from Laau Point on Molokai to Hawaii Kai on Oahu ends the season. The race draws an annually increasing number of skilled international competitors.

Touring the Islands in inflatable kayaks is an irresistible attraction for many outdoor enthusiasts. There are several organizations and outdoor guides that lead kayak, hiking and camping tours along the Islands' deserted coastlines and into their unpopulated valleys.

Although *swimming* is the most popular participation sport in the United States, some Mainland waters are just too cold for anything but a quick dip. But not Hawaii's. All of Hawaii's beaches are public and accessible by right of way; year-around sun worshippers crowd the shores. And the 70- to 80-degree waters teem with swimmers of all ages.

Hawaii is home for the Uluniu Swim Club, oldest women's swimming club in the United States. Founded in 1909, its stated objective was »to encourage swimming and surfing and to provide recreational facilities for the enjoyment of the beach.« Another objective was to encourage women's participation in water sports. When the club was 54 years old, it rewrote its rules and admitted men as full voting members.

Hawaii has had its share of internationally famous swimming champions, including Olympic gold medalists Duke Paoa Kahanamoku and Ford Kono. Countless numbers of swimmers are involved in the sport today. Hundreds of age-group students compete interscholastically or for private swim clubs, while adults swim daily for fitness or fun.

Competitive ocean events increase annually. The largest and most famous race is the annual Labor Day Waikiki Roughwater Swim, a 2.375-mile race from Sans Souci Beach at the Diamond Head end of Waikiki to Duke Kahanamoku Beach at the Hilton Hawaiian Village.

Inaugurated in 1969 with a handful of swimmers, the race now draws an international field of approximately 1,200 competitors from ages 8 to 80. Other popular swimming events include: the 1-mile Hapuna Rough Water ocean swim on the Big Island; the Maui Channel Swim, a 10-mile Lanai-to-Maui, six-person relay; Oahu's 2.4-mile North Shore Challenge; and the 5-mile Possibly Annual Hawaiian Christmas *Looong* Distance Invitational Rough H_2O Swim, also on Oahu.

In November 1983 the rest of the nation shivered under a blanket of snow while 36 men and 36 women, a virtual who's who of American swimming, spent two weeks at camp in sunny Honolulu. They were preparing for the Olympic trials. The coaching staff of the 1984 U.S. Olympic team drilled them relentlessly at the University of Hawaii's Duke Kahanamoku swimming pool and training facility. It was the first camp of its kind for members of United States Swimming Inc. (USSI).

There are four Interscholastic League of Honolulu schools competing in *water polo* and several local players have earned water polo scholarships at Mainland colleges. In 1984, intercollegiate water polo made a comeback in Hawaii when Chaminade University formed a team. Also, there are a number of private clubs enjoying the sport.

Among the most popular water sports attractions for visitors are *diving* and *snorkeling*. Recreational scuba diving is available through dive tours, and Hawaii, with its dazzling underwater world of tropical fish and coral, ranks near the top as a prime destination for divers.

Although *surfing*, the »sport of kings,« traveled north from southern Polynesia to the Islands, it is considered Hawaii's gift to the world. In ancient times surfing was interwoven into Hawaiian culture and, along with other popular sports of the day, played an important role in many seasonal celebrations. Later, when the missionaries dominated Island customs, surfing was all but forgotten.
When Alexander Hume Ford leased a section of Waikiki Beach from Queen Liliuokalani and founded the Outrigger Canoe Club in 1908, surfing was reborn. From then on, the classic image of Hawaii was Diamond Head and surfers on a Waikiki wave. Slow to move from the gentle rollers of Waikiki Beach, surfing finally reached the bigger waves of Makaha in the early 1930s. In 1953, the Waikiki Surf Club held the first International Surfing Championships at Makaha Beach and the sport became an international phenomenon. Today Buffalo's Big Board Surfing Classic, an event with equal amounts of amateur surfing and professional Island entertainment, has replaced the Makaha meet.
The Gotcha Pro, a professional contest sanctioned by the Association of Surfing Professionals (ASP), made its debut in 1986 at Sandy Beach. The first professional meet ever held in the summertime on Oahu's south shore, it was the largest surf meet in Hawaii.
December's Triple Crown of Surfing, also ASP events, showcases professionally ranked international surfers in The Billabong Pro, The Marui/Offshore Masters Surfing Championship and the World Cup of Surfing for men and women. All three take place in December's huge winter surf on Oahu's North Shore – the undisputed big wave capital of the world.
The Hawaiian Surfing Association (HSA) is a 2,000-member organization with districts on every island. Each district holds five contests a year and there is a state meet in August. Once every four years the amateur national championships are held in Hawaii.

Surfing is also an interscholastic sport, with contests from spring until the national championships in August. The National Scholastic Surfing Association (NSSA), has districts on each island for all full-time students.

Windsurfers, or sailboards, were invented in the United States. But the sport flourished only in Europe until a young 13-year old named Robby Naish, from Oahu, won a world championship with skills he'd developed battling the tradewinds of Kailua Bay. Now Mainland and European boardsailors recognize Hawaii, especially Hookipa Beach on Maui, as the mecca of high wind and waves, the perfect place for windsurfing.
Many European sailboard instructors and competitive sailors reside in Hawaii, or at least spend their winters here, polishing their high-wind, high-wave performances. According to them, Hawaii is the source of all the windsurfing innovations, new equipment, new sail and board designs and new maneuvers.
Scheduled weekend races and major professional windsurfing contests take place on Oahu and Maui throughout the year. Two favorite wave-jumping sites are Oahu's Kuilei Cliffs Beach Park beneath the towering peak of Diamond Head and Hookipa Beach Park on Maui's windward shore. Kailua Bay offers a high-wind training ground offshore, while small waves and calm waters inshore make it a favorite place for beginners to learn this fastest growing sport in the Islands.

Bodysurfing, the art of riding a wave with your body from a point off shore in to the beach, is a purist sport utilizing only the body, a wave and swim fins. Most bodysurfers consider Makapuu on Oahu's eastern shore one of their favorite bodysurfing sites. Sandy Beach and the North Shore also offer excellent bodysurfing.
In December 1980 the first professional bodysurfing contest was held at Banzai Pipeline, on Oahu's North Shore. In February 1981 the Halona Point Bodysurfing Association, the Honolulu Bodysurfing Club and the Makapuu Bodysurfing Association joined to form the Hawaiian Bodysurfing Association (HBA) in order to promote a pro/am contest circuit for the Islands.

Bodyboarding is a relatively new water sport that utilizes a high-speed planing device made of inexpensive and lightweight foam. Easier to ride than a surfboard, a bodyboard can be mastered relatively quickly and does not require perfect waves. Bodyboards first appeared about 1972 and the number of people now enjoying the sport has been growing ever since. In 1983 the

Hawaiian Bodyboarding Association (HBA) was formed to organize pro/am contests, and an international championship is now held annually at the Pipeline.

From those who throw their nets off lava shores, to crab fishermen dangling traps off bridges, to youngsters with bamboo poles, or anglers trolling with expensive rods and reels on power boats offshore, *fishing* for relaxation and pleasure is a popular Island sport. Ancient Hawaiian fishing was a mixture of superstition and science. Because of the variety of ethnic backgrounds and diverse cultural heritages, most of the fishing methods evolved in Hawaii through the ages are different from those in other parts of the world. Even the fish have different names and habits. Today Hawaii fishing is a high-tech affair – but the superstitions still remain. For example, few Hawaii fishermen will ever leave shore without a ti leaf tucked away somewhere on the boat, and Hawaii fishermen never carry bananas on board.

Jackpot fishing tournaments from early spring until late fall offer large cash purses, new automobiles and other merchandise, luring anglers from around the world.

The annual Hawaiian International Billfish Tournament (billfish includes several species, not all are found in Hawaiian waters) was first held in Kailua-Kona on the Big Island in 1958. The HIBT is an amateur competition thought to be the oldest fishing tournament in the Pacific. It draws celebrities, royalty and world record holders, bringing together more top anglers at one time and in one place than any other tournament. The largest billfish ever caught in the HIBT was a 1,062-1/2-pound Pacific blue marlin boated by Gil Kraemer in the 1986 event.

The largest fish ever caught on rod and reel, a 1,805-pound Pacific blue marlin, was boated off Oahu by Capt. Cornelius Choy. The largest marlin caught off Kailua-Kona is a 1,656-pound blue, landed by Gary Merriman fishing aboard *Black Bart* in 1984.

Although fresh-water fishing in Hawaii has received little attention, the sport does have its enthusiasts. The Division of Aquatic Resources initiated a program to introduce desirable fresh-water game fish into the perennial streams of the Islands. Nine species, including rainbow trout, are now firmly established and providing good fishing.

There are four state-regulated and managed fresh-water public fishing areas on Kauai, Oahu and Hawaii. Licenses are required and are valid for one year, from July until June.

Strong trade winds, warm tropical waters and balmy temperatures make Hawaii a year-round *sailing* paradise. Both racing and cruising are popular. The 19 chartered yacht clubs, all members of the Hawaii Yacht Racing Association, hold races each week for every kind of craft. Each island offers sheltered anchorage for hundreds of cruisers who call daily from foreign ports.

In the 1880s King Kalakaua took up sailing, and yachting became a principal Hawaiian sport. Mark Twain, Robert Louis Stevenson, Jack London, Gen. George Patton and Shirley Temple, have all played a part in Hawaii's diverse sailing history. Dennis Conner and the *Stars & Stripes* America's Cup challengers trained for the 1987 America's Cup Challenges off Hawaii's shores. The training paid off; Conner and crew brought home the Cup.

The first Trans-Pacific Yacht Race happened in 1906 when Honolulu sailor Clarence Macfarlane sailed to San Francisco and later raced back 2,500 miles from San Pedro to Honolulu. The event, now held every other year, is the oldest major distance yacht race in the world and the oldest organized sporting event in Hawaii.

The newest yachting event, the Kenwood Cup Hawaii International Ocean Racing Series, was inaugurated in 1978 as the Pan Am Clipper Cup. It was eventually acclaimed one of the five most prestigious yacht race series in the world and was re-named in 1986. It is held every even-numbered year and features five challenging races: three 27-mile Olympic triangles off Waikiki; a middle-distance 150-mile race along the North Shore of Molokai; and a 775-mile Around-the-State race. Hawaii is, of course, the only place a boat can sail around an entire state.

In 1973 the University of Hawaii sailing team won the Douglas Cup, bringing Hawaii its first national championship in any sport. Dozens of national and world championship competitions, in both monohull and multi-hull designs, have been held here. In 1976, Honolulu Tornado sailors Dave McFaull and Mike Rothwell won a silver medal in the Montreal Olympics.

Where can you sail in tropical breezes all morning and *snow ski* all afternoon? In Hawaii, on the craggy, frozen slopes of Mauna Kea – a 13,796-foot dormant volcano on the Big Island.

The »mountain« offers varying ski conditions with temperatures ranging from 35 to 60 degrees Fahrenheit. For beginners there's Poi Bowl, a three-quarter-mile run with a 400- to 500-foot vertical drop. To ski Pele's Power, a north-facing slope, you have to take a hike first, and for the experienced skier, the King Kamehameha run features a 1,000-foot drop in less than three quarters of a mile. Warrior's Run simply goes down into a gulch.

Occasionally, good storms dump plenty of snow on this tropical Everest. In a big snowfall, the snow holds down to 11,000 feet, with runs of as much as 3 to 5 miles. Snow can come as early as November and last until June; some years it doesn't snow at all. But that doesn't discourage members of the Ski Association of Hawaii (SAH) who simply travel someplace else when it doesn't snow here.

Annual competitions (when there's snow) include: the Aloha Cup for beginning and intermediate skiers; the Hawaii Ski Cup, open Alpine and Nordic combined runs; the Mauna Kea Cup, a cross-country race; and Pele's Cup.

Conditions on Mauna Kea are primitive: no snow blower to clear the roads, no lift, no accommodations. Frequently skiers and astronomers from the University of Hawaii Institute of Astronomy (located at the top of the mountain) are snowed out.

The inaugural training camp for the 1984 U. S. Women's Olympic Ski team was not held on the snow-packed slopes of a Mainland ski resort but on the sun-baked shores and pasture land of Huehue Ranch on the Big Island. Designed to build mental toughness and deliberately located away from a traditional ski environment, the summer camp included ocean swimming, trail running, biking, tennis, canoe paddling, volleyball and weightlifting.

Mauna Kea and other mountain areas in the Islands offer a variety of recreational pursuits, including *game hunting*. For many people, hunting is a unique way to enjoy the beauty, peace and solitude of the Islands. More than 13,000 hunters participate in the sport annually.

The Hawaii Rifle Association (HRA) was established on Oahu in 1857. Its activities include gun collecting, competitive shooting and hunting. Members organize programs to promote rifle marksmanship and hold annual deer hunting tournaments.

The Division of Forestry and Wildlife maintains public areas on six of the islands, where bird and mammal hunting is available to the general public during specific seasons. Hunters may use rifles, bows and arrows and dogs. Sixteen species of birds and seven species of mammals are on the list of open game.

Hunters of certain big game species on public lands are selected or assigned by public drawing. Hunting on private lands is permitted by permission of the land owner. All hunters must have a valid state of Hawaii hunting license and all firearms brought into Hawaii must be registered within 48 hours of arrival.

One of the best ways to see the Islands close up and get in touch with nature is through *hiking, backpacking* and *camping*.

Except for Mauna Loa, Mauna Kea and Haleakala, the mountains of Hawaii are comparatively low by standards of other areas, but the terrain is rugged. There are jagged peaks, precipitous cliffs and crumbly rock. Lava that is merciless on footwear sometimes conceals beneath its thin crust tubes or holes into which an unwary hiker might fall. On green mountains the vegetation can be so dense that hikers who stray off the trail may become exhausted while trying to find their way back. Green ridges and wet valleys often hold plenty of mud. In dry areas there are thorny plants and prickly cactus.

But there are no snakes or poison ivy in Hawaii and the Island climate makes hiking a year-round activity.

Solitary hiking is dangerous, so the best way to become acqainted with Hawaii's forests is through the weekly hikes led by the Trail and Mountain Club or the Sierra Club. Hiking maps of every island are available and many of the most popular treks are designated trails in county, state and federal parks. Cabins for camping in some parks are available by reservation. There are also historic trails through ancient Hawaiian sites.

Following in the footsteps of hiking – but at a faster pace – are *jogging* and *running*, two sports that have taken over the Islands. Although no official statistics are available, Hawaii claims more runners per capita than any other state in the union. Night or day, wherever you look, there are runners.

Each year more and more foot races are added to an already crowded calendar. Often as many as two or three races of varying distances are held every weekend. Some of these are: the Honolulu Women Runners 10 K, an all women's race; the annual Honolulu Marathon, third largest in the United States; the 87-mile Saddle Road Run from Hilo to Waimea; and the Run to the Sun, a 37-mile climb from sea level up 10,000 feet to Maui's Haleakala crater.

Hawaii residents respect their volcanoes but are not afraid of them. So when there is an eruption, people don't flee but instead run *to* the volcano to watch the lava flow. Hence, the currently active Kilauea on the slopes of Mauna Loa is sometimes called a »drive-in volcano.«

Supposedly, bad luck haunts souvenir hunters who remove lava rock from Hawaii. But there are no superstitions about running on lava rock. The Kilauea Volcano Wilderness Marathon and Rim Runs, three different events held at an altitude of 4,000 feet at Hawaii Volcanoes National Park, have runners doing just that.

The race is subject to cancellation if the volcano erupts.

The Wilderness Marathon is considered one of the toughest runs in the world. Recommended for hardy athletes only, it takes runners over a primordial landscape that includes *a'a* and *pahoehoe* lava under foot and sulfur-scented steam rising from subterranean vents. The 10-mile Summit Caldera Run crosses portions of the most recent volcanic eruptions. The 5-mile Kilauea Iki Crater Run descends from Thurston Lava Tube into *'ohia* tree-fern forests on the crater floor and across the crusted-over lava pond of the 1959 eruption.

Organized and staffed by volunteer forest rangers from the National Park Service and the Volcano Arts Center, the three events are the only foot races in the U.S. held within the confines of a national park. Sheraton Volcano House has unfurnished cabins available for those who like to camp before or after the runs.

Hawaii, Maui, Kauai and Oahu have stables for boarding or renting horses. Some stables include rings for riding lessons or for practicing equestrian techniques. Guided *horseback rides* from Koko Crater Stables on Oahu take you through a botanical garden of arid plants. On Maui, trail rides lead into the West Maui Mountains. The Big Island's rides take the equestrians through desertlike *paniolo* (cowboy) country; and on Kauai the trails lead into the mountains of the state forest reserve.

When not leading trail rides or working at other jobs, many paniolos compete in Hawaii's rodeo circuit – bulldogging, calf-roping and bronc riding their way from island to island.

There is also a solid corps of *polo* players in Hawaii. As in many other Hawaii sporting events, polo has attracted international competition. Prince Charles played polo in Hawaii in the '70s. Each year five or six foreign teams are invited to compete at the Mokuleia polo club.

Bike riding's popularity continues to grow in the Islands. The Hawaii Bicycling League (HBL) conducts Sunday outings on Oahu for riders of all abilities and frequently leads tours to the neighboring islands. Heavy automobile traffic and a lack of bike paths can be discouraging, and while some visitors like to bike tour and camp, bike travel and camping by oneself is not recommended.

Century rides are held each spring and fall. Since 1982, the September Century ride, sanctioned by the National League of American Wheelmen, organized by the Hawaii Bicycling League (HBL) and sponsored by *The Honolulu Advertiser*, has been the largest such event in the U.S. More than 2,000 riders rise before dawn and brave 80-degree heat to ride their chosen 25, 50 or 100 miles.

There are bike racing clubs on Oahu, Maui and Hawaii. The season runs from January to November and competition ranges from short, fast criterium racing to longer time trials and road races. The two longest bike competitions are the 112-mile Dick Evans Memorial race around Oahu and the Kona Coast Century, a 100-mile race on the Ironman triathlon course.

It isn't often that a new event in the world of sports rewrites sports history. But that's exactly what happened when the Ironman, a 2.4-mile swim/112-mile bike ride/26.2-mile run *triathlon* hit the Islands in 1978.

A triathlon combines these three single sports into one consecutive race. Prior to the Ironman a few short triathlons drew small fields in California, but the only multi-sport event in Hawaii was a short-distance run/swim biathlon co-sponsored by the Mid Pacific Road Runners Club (MPRRC) and the Waikiki Swim Club. In 1977 John Collins, a Navy commander and a member of MPRRC, came up with the idea of combining the Waikiki Roughwater Swim, the Around-Oahu Bike Race and the Honolulu Marathon. He claimed anybody who could finish such a race would certainly be made of iron.

For the first two years, only 15 people entered. Except for a *Sports Illustrated* writer who wrote a 1979 feature about it, nobody other than a few family members and friends paid much attention to the race. Then in 1980, 108 athletes entered and ABC-TV's Wide World of Sports filmed the event. People began to take notice. Most concluded that anyone who would attempt such a race was absolutely crazy.

In 1981 the Ironman Triathlon moved to Kailua-Kona on the Big Island, where it is now held each October. Entries are limited to 1,000 athletes but they come from all over the world. The race and the influx of people add millions of dollars to the Big Island economy. The Ironman has become ABC's most successful sports program. Because of its media appeal, unequalled growth and splendid location, the Ironman is one of Hawaii's major international competitions. Because of the long distances, unrelenting heat and the difficult lava course, it is called the world's toughest endurance event.

Today there are short-course and long-distance triathlons on every island. The most popular short-course race is July's Tinman Triathlon on Oahu which draws 1,100 triathletes.

Soaring (or gliding, as it is often called) takes place on Oahu's North Shore. Members of the Civil Air Patrol, Honolulu Soaring Club and Oahu Soaring Club take off from Dillingham Field for long, silent trips above the cliffs and out over the ocean. Several club members who are licensed glider pilots offer lessons and take passengers up for rides.

This does not exhaust the list of Hawaii's outdoor sports, of course. Others, alphabetically, are: acrobatics, archery (Japanese and American style), auto racing, basketball, cricket, dirt bike riding, fencing, football, Frisbee throwing, go-carting, golf, hang gliding, horseshoes, jet skiing, juggling, kite flying, lawn bowling, moto-cross, paddle boarding, para-sailing, radio controlled model boats and cars, roller skating, rugby, skateboarding, skeet shooting, sky diving, soccer, softball, tennis, volleyball and water skiing.

Most important, Hawaii outdoor sports know no season. Every day is an outdoor day in Hawaii, so if you're looking for something to do, step outside. You will never be bored.

ISLAND FLORA: A UNIQUE, FRAGILE GARDEN by Carolyn A. Corn

he Hawaiian Islands have undergone a fascinating evolution of plant and animal life. Probably nowhere else in the world has a comparable area become such a showcase of evolutionary processes. Comparably bizarre living forms, many on the verge of extinction, interact to create a unique native flora. The gentle islands are known for their beauty and mild weather, yet few visitors know the fascinating story which makes these islands so unique.

Because the islands have a volcanic origin, plants could not establish themselves until after the hot lava broke through the ocean's surface and began to cool. Some plants came early, maybe 30 million years ago, others arrived much later. Since these islands have always been isolated from other high islands and continents by thousands of miles of ocean, only certain plant propagules could survive long-distance travel over, on or through the ocean. The most probable means of arrival for many native land plants is by birds, either by means of exterior attachment of the seeds and propagules, or by their being eaten and carried internally. Wind dispersal of small seeds, moss and fern spores is also likely. Marine algae and some land plants, particularly strand plants, may have arrived at the islands through or on the ocean's surface.

Chance played an important role in the successful establishment of these colonizing species. Not only did the arriving propagules have to be alive, but they had to be desposited or land in a spot where they could grow. Those from a similar maritime habitat had the best chance of surviving, but only certain plants could reproduce themselves and avoid extinction. Plant pollinators, which also had to come from outside, were not always present. Thus only certain kinds of plants arrived here able to survive and become the ancestors of Hawaii's native plant flora.

The first land surfaces available for plants to colonize were the oldest islands, located northwest of the present high islands. The islands as they first formed were low in elevation and could support only coastal vegetation. Then as volcanic activity added to their height and size, the islands were able to support additional habitats and a variety of plants. Wind and water began to erode the shield-shaped volcanic cones into valleys, ridges and cliffs. These newer, often windy habitats provided additional specialized places for plants.

In the meantime, new islands to the southeast became high islands with many climatic and edaphic (soil) habitats available for plants to colonize. Most of the flora for these islands probably arrived from propa-

gules of nearby islands, although some could also have arrived from outside the Hawaiian chain. Thus, as new islands formed, colonizing species could hopscotch from older to newer islands and avoid extinction. Over time, the oldest islands weathered until little or no volcanic surface was above sea level and they could no longer support more than a strand of coastal vegetation. Currently these low islands form the Northwestern Hawaiian Islands, and the high islands to the southeast, the main Hawaiian Islands, now have the greatest number of habitats and plant species.

Some ancestral plants did not evolve into new species, while others proliferated into many species, varieties and forms which were adapted to various and sometimes specialized habitats. For instance, on one island three or four ancestral cyrtandra species are thought to have given rise to over 300 different kinds of modern day plants, many of which occur only along one valley or ridge top. From as few as 275 original ancestral plants, Hawaii today has a native flora of about 2,400 different kinds of flowering plants. Many occur within restricted geographic, climatic and/or edaphic habitats.

Although Hawaiian marine plants are quite similar to those of neighboring archipelagoes, the land plants are often unique. About 45 percent of the moss, 71 percent of the fern and 96 percent of the flowering plant taxa in Hawaii are endemic (occur naturally nowhere else in the world). These exceptional plants form a distinctive flora that serves as a home and food source for equally unique native insects and birds.

Because of the islands' evolutionary history and isolation, the native flora lacks certain elements one would expect to find within a comparable continental area. For example, there are no native representatives in plant families like mangrove, ginger, banana, pineapple and cactus, and no native conifers like pine trees. Hawaii has fewer native orchids than any other state. Native vines and herbs are poorly represented, as are the rose, mustard and palm families. An extra number of species are present in the gloxinia, composite, lobelia and coffee families. This flora has been called disharmonic because it has gaps that allow recent plant introductions a chance to naturalize themselves very effectively within these native ecosystems.

The uniform maritime climate permits year-around plant growth. Over the centuries some species have become large and woody when compared to closely related plants outside Hawaii. For instance, the silversword, which is related to a small tarweed on the west coast of North America, has evolved into a large alpine species in Hawaii. It grows for a number of years as a globose cluster of succulent silvery leaves whose stem then elongates and flowers once in spectacular splendor before the plant dies. There are also tree lobelias, thistle trees, tree geraniums, shrubby violets, tree gardenias, bush chickweeds and specialized lobelias that look like a head of cabbage perched upon a bowling-pin-shaped trunk.

Since Hawaii plants evolved without grazing mammals, the majority did not develop botanical defenses like thorns, stinging hairs, toxic qualities or bad tastes. Few species are fire tolerant and they often have shallow root systems. This makes them very vulnerable to grazing animals, which were introduced into the islands a little over 200 years ago, and to the feral Polynesian pigs.

The upper canopy of most native forest ecosystems is dominated by only one or two species. The most common native tree is the 'ohia which grows from sea level to tree line in wet or dry forests on the six largest islands. It is highly variable in appearance and may bloom as a shrub when less than 1 foot tall in wet bogs, or it may become a tall tree on deep ash soils. On exposed ridges, cliffs and in dry forests it grows as a small tree or shrub. Not only does it colonize barren lava flows, it also germinates in wet forests as an epiphyte on tree ferns, and after its roots reach the ground, it may displace or strangle the tree fern. The attractive flower clusters are usually red in color, but may also be pink, orange or, infrequently, yellow or chartreuse. Like other myrtaceous plants the flowers look like shaving brushes because of their showy, numerous stamens. The flower nectar serves as a vital year-around food source for forest birds and insects. A number of Hawaiian legends refer to this tree whose wood was used for *poi* boards, house timbers, idols, *kapa* (bark-cloth) beaters and enclosures about temples. The flowers, young leaves, buds and capsules are used to make *leis*. The dense, red wood is sometimes used as lumber; the narrow boards make a very attractive floor that is highly termite resistent.

A dominant tree in mesic forests is the *koa*. This majestic tree grows to be a monarch in mid-elevation forests, where under ideal conditions it may reach to 140 feet in height. Once common on the six main islands, its numbers have been reduced because of habitat alterations and logging. The rich brown wood, which has rippled and curly grain patterns, is highly valued for making furniture, floors, carved bowls and bookends. In 'Iolani Palace, many items, including the beautiful central staircase, are made from koa. The Hawaiians utilized the straight trees to make outrigger canoes, surfboards, house timbers, bearing sticks, *kahili* handles, paddles and spears. The koa provides a home for many native insects, and these insects are an important food source for native birds.

In the same legume family as the koa, a smaller tree called the *mamane* grows at middle to upper altitudes on the six main islands. It is common, however, only on Maui and Hawaii, where there is more land at higher altitudes. The nectar from its yellow blossoms and the seeds in the immature pods are the primary food source for the endangered *palila* bird. The very durable, hard yellow wood was used by the Hawaiians for house timbers, sled runners and Hawaiian spades. It also makes an excellent fire, burning quietly with a pleasing aroma.

Within the rain forest the lacy fronds of the tree fern are conspicuous beneath the 'ohia trees. Birds utilize the tree ferns as nesting sites; feral pigs consume the starchy interior of the stems. Portions of the stem are also used as a medium to grow anthuriums and orchids, and occasionally the young frond shoots are boiled and eaten by humans. Prior to the manufacture of synthetics, the golden fibers of some tree ferns were used to stuff pillows and beds. In times of famine, Hawaiians would bake and eat the soft core of the fern trunk.

The 'ohia, koa, mamane and tree fern are common components of Hawaiian forests. In addition, there are many species which occur only on limited geographic, climatic, historic and edaphic sites. For a moment, let us try to picture the islands prior to the arrival of man, about 300 A.D. All the vegetation is native and the ecosystems generally reflect the climatic zones. These zones may form complete or incomplete bands around the islands at different elevations. If the island is high, one will ascend through a series of ecosystems starting at the coast and going inland from coastal shrub, mesic (moderate moisture) forest, then rain forest and bogs at middle altitudes. As one goes higher the rain forest again gives way to a mesic then xeric (low moisture) vegetation. The treeline, which may be as high as 8,500 feet in elevation, gives way to lower shrubs. Xeric and freezing conditions prevail with flowering plants, grasses, lichens and mosses becoming scarce above 10,000 feet altitude. The tops of the highest mountains, Mauna Kea and Mauna Loa on the Big Island, are essentially rocky deserts which receive periodic snow. A similar zonation is present on the leeward side of the island and on mountains located in the rain shadow of higher mountains; however, a dry forest becomes a significant feature at middle altitudes.

If no mountains block the trade winds, rain forests and bogs occur between 2,000 and 5,300 feet altitude. On poorly drained soils, stunted bog vegetation may occur within the rain forest. Where the soil is bet-

Taro fields cover most of Kauai's Hanalei Valley floor. These plants with edible roots, which the Polynesians brought to Hawaii in their canoes, were their favorite food staple.

Mountain apples may have been the first fruit brought to Hawaii by the early Polynesian settlers. Mountain apples still grow in Waipio Valley on the Big Island.

As in early times, part of this huge valley is covered with taro fields irrigated by the waters of 1,000-foot Hi'ilawe Falls.

The ancient Hawaiians burned the oil-rich nuts of the *kukui* (candlenut tree) like candles for illumination. They made dyes for kapa cloth from the nuts, bark and roots.

The kukui, with its distinctive silver leaves, is the state tree of Hawaii.

All parts of the coconut palm had an important use for the

Hawaiians: the coconut for food, drink and body oil; the leaves for woven mats; the trunk for hula drums; and the roots for fish baskets and traps.

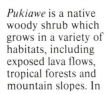 *Pukiawe* is a native woody shrub which grows in a variety of habitats, including exposed lava flows, tropical forests and mountain slopes. In ancient Hawaii, smoke from burning pukiawe wood was used in purification ceremonies.

White-blooming ginger was brought to Hawaii by early Polynesian settlers and cultivated for a variety of medicines and other uses.

 The hibiscus is the official flower of the state of Hawaii. Mostly garden ornamentals, hibiscus are hybrids; there are an estimated 5,000 varieties. Native hibiscus are uncommon, but they do occur in a variety of colors.

This unique 6½-foot tall silversword, native to Maui, blooms as an alpine plant at the 9,500-foot level on the western side of Haleakala Crater. Depending on local conditions, the silversword grows as a cluster of succulent silvery leaves from 4 to 20 years, then shoots up a spectacular flower spike, sets seeds and dies. At an altitude of 10,023 feet, Haleakala Crater measures 3 miles by 7 miles, one of the largest calderas in the world. A rift running across the crater's floor is marked by a line of multi-colored symmetrical cinder cones. Haleakala Crater is now a national park.

Sugar cane and pineapple on the sunny slopes of West Maui mountains near Kapalua. Although the Polynesian settlers brought sugar cane with them, it was the white man who introduced the commercial cane in the middle of the last century. Pineapple was introduced from South America at the turn of the century. For a long time, both products have been the backbone of Hawaii's economy.

When sugar cane is mature, the leaves are burned in the fields and the sugar bearing stalks are transported to the mills.

On the islands of Oahu, Maui and Lanai, large fields of uniform rows of pineapple with its gray-green leaves cover the landscape. Keeping records of growth, this female inspector wears protective clothing against insects and the sharp spines at the tips of the pineapple leaves.

Besides sugar cane and pineapple, other agricultural products are also vital to Hawaii's economy. Papaya, a most delicious tropical fruit, grows at lower elevations in many parts of the state with the largest orchards on the Big Island.

The Kona area of the Big Island is the only place in the United States where coffee is now commercially grown. Hand-picked between October and January when the beans are turning red, Kona coffee is highly regarded for its robust flavor.

Originally imported from Australia, macadamia nuts today are grown on more than 12,000 acres on the Big Island. These nuts possess fine flavor and can be eaten raw or roasted.

Cattle herding on a Molokai ranch.

Branding cattle on the Kukaiau Ranch on the slopes of Mauna Kea. Cowboys are called *paniolo*, after the »Espanols« (Spaniards), brought to Hawaii by King Kamehameha III in the 1830s to teach the Hawaiians cattle-herding skills.

Paniolo Chipper Chapple rides a bull at the annual Great Waikoloa Rodeo and Horserace at South Kohala on the Big Island. Cowboys come from all over the state, and even the Mainland, to compete.

The ancient lava flows off the Kohala mountains now offer fertile soil for ranching. The biggest Island spread of them all is Parker Ranch, with around 225,000 acres, one of the largest ranches in the United States under single ownership. Neighboring Monte Richards Ranch has installed batteries of modern windmills to produce the electricity needed for ranch operations.

The upper canopy of the native forest along Kauai's Pihea trail is dominated by 'ohia trees. The wood of the 'ohia was often carved into temple images in ancient times. The trail follows the rim of the spectacular Kalalau Valley, located north of Waimea Canyon, on the way to Alaka'i swamp, home of endangered native birds. Gold trees and rainbow shower trees are introduced species and found throughout the Islands. Their blossoms add yet another accent to the infinite mosaic of year-round colors of Hawaii.

POLITICS AND ECONOMICS: STRENGTH THROUGH DIVERSITY by Dan Boylan

A visitor to the Islands in the midst of an election campaign could readily see that Hawaii's citizens play a unique brand of politics. Consider the Hawaii campaign ritual of political sign-waving. In order to preserve Hawaii's beauty, the state long ago banned billboard advertising. In the late 1960s Island political candidates, hungry for name recognition among the voters, began making human billboards of themselves. Today, candidates for every office from state legislator to county mayor array themselves and their supporters along Hawaii's highways, mornings and evenings, for months on end, holding political signs and waving at passing motorists.

Or consider the opening day of the state Legislature in January. A visitor need only observe that day's proceedings to know that the aloha spirit of love, friendship and cooperation extends to Island politics. Senators and state representatives sit in their respective chambers, festooned with flower leis, listening to Island musicians and watching Hawaiian dancers. Later, each legislator holds an opening day reception in his or her office for any citizen who cares to stop by. Island delicacies from Hawaiian *laulau* (fish or pork wrapped in banana leaves) to Japanese *sushi* to Filipino *adobo* (pork or chicken cooked in a vinegar sauce) laden tables set for the legislator's constituents.

If a visitor looks closely at the legislative menus and at the faces of those waving by the roadsides, he may well discover the central fact of Hawaii's political life: Hawaii knows only minorities. No single ethnic group dominates the society. Caucasians make up 27 percent of the population, Japanese 23 percent, Filipinos 11 percent and Chinese 5 percent. Fully 28 percent of the Islands' population is of mixed parentage, including most of those who identify themselves as Hawaiians. In all, 27 different ethnic groups interact to give the Islands their colorful and distinct social fabric.

Nowhere is Hawaii's rich ethnic diversity more apparent than in the Islands' politics. Since Hawaii became a state in 1959, its voters have sent two Japanese, a Chinese and a Caucasian to the United States Senate. The state's two seats in the United States House of Representatives have belonged to two Caucasians, four Japanese and a Hawaiian.

Political power on the state level reflects an even more diverse ethnic mix. Two Caucasians, a Japanese and a Hawaiian have held Hawaii's governorship. Its lieutenant governorship, the second highest elective office in the state, has been filled by three Hawaiians, a Chinese, a Caucasian, a Japanese, a Caucasian-Japanese and a Filipino. The 25-member state Senate and 51-member state House of Representatives look like some sort of Pacific Rim regional conference. The legislative roster includes two Hondas, two Wongs, two Iges, a Kanoha, a Lee, a Fukunaga, an Okamura, a Medeiros, a Marumoto and a Cachola.

Hawaii's multi-ethnic Legislature is an expression of the Islands' commitment to political egalitarianism. It is one thing to promise, as the United States has since its inception, political equality for all. It is quite another to extend it, as Hawaii has, to citizens representing most of the culturally diverse states of Asia and the Pacific. The latter constitutes a significant assertion of the democratic faith.

Its ethnic variety lends Hawaii's politics their fascination. I doubt that there's anything like it anywhere else in the world. Modern American political campaigns require raising vast sums of money, fashioning positions on the major issues of the day and organizing workers to get out the candidate's or party's message. In Hawaii every political campaign is also an exercise in putting together a sufficient number of ethnic blocs to give you a majority vote.

That's never easy. It requires marrying cultural groups that often have very little in common, save rice as a staple. It produces party slates designed specifically to attract broad-based ethnic support. In 1986, for example, the Democratic Party produced a textbook lesson in Island coalition-building. The Democrats offered a Japanese for the United States Senate, a Samoan for the U. S. House of Representatives, a Hawaiian for governor and a Filipino for lt. governor. One political observer called it a »rainbow coalition.« Indeed, it was.

Island politics is ostensibly organized by the Democratic and Republican parties. Seldom in the history of the state and territory, however, have the two parties been competitive. Throughout most of the Territorial period, from 1900 to 1959, a coalition of Caucasian, Hawaiian and Chinese voters allowed the Republican party to dominate the Legislature and the only Territory-wide elective office, the delegateship to the U. S. Congress.

In the early 1950s an emerging Japanese-American population combined with Hawaii's principal labor unions behind the Democratic standard. The Democrats seized legislative power in 1954, and they have never relinquished it. Since statehood in 1959, the Republican Party has held the governorship (William F. Quinn) for only one abbreviated term. Hiram Fong, a Republican of Chinese ancestry, held a U. S. Senate seat for 17 years, and in 1986 Hawaii's voters sent their first Republican to the United States House of Representatives. Otherwise, Island politics has belonged to the Democrats.

In the absence of sufficient competition between parties, interest groups wield enormous power in executive and legislative offices. Island lawmakers listen attentively to the concerns of lobbyists for the tourist industry, the sugar and pineapple producers, and the construction industry – all three mainstays of Hawaii's economy.

Organized labor also plays a pivotal role. After World War II, the International Longshoremen and Warehousemen's Union, representing Hawaii's sugar and pineapple workers, lobbied hard in the territorial and state Legislatures for enactment of progressive labor legislation. Over the past quarter century, the numbers and consequently the political clout of blue collar labor has markedly diminished. In its stead, white collar unions of government employees and schoolteachers have come to play an increasingly powerful political role.

Ethnic bloc-voting and one-party rule alone fail to explain fully the uniqueness of Hawaii's political culture. Island politicians, for example, simply do not conform to the national stereotype. They neither slap backs nor orate long-windedly. Few play to the television cameras or the newspapers. Instead, they demonstrate the sense of reserve in which they were reared or to which they have become accustomed.

Consider, for example, the state's three Democratic governors: John Burns (1962–74), George Ariyoshi (1974–86) and John Waihee (1986–). Burns was a consummate political organizer who probably understood the state's problems and its people better than any man who's ever held the office. But Burns shunned the press and did little to advertise himself or his accomplishments.

George Ariyoshi is a tall, handsome *nisei* (second-generation Japanese in Hawaii) with a law degree from the University of Michigan. In his 32-year career in elective politics, he never lost an election.

Yet Ariyoshi remains a shy man. During his final term as governor, I watched him address a memorial gathering of the all-Japanese-American 100th Battalion Club at the National Memorial Cemetery of the Pacific in Punchbowl. The audience belonged to him. They shared his ethnicity and were of his age. Of the 500 men and women in attendance, there were probably less than three dozen who had not voted for him in his last election campaign. Many had given him not only their votes but their time and money as well.

Yet Ariyoshi was obviously uncomfortable in their midst. At the reception following the service, he stood at the edge of the crowd. He shook few hands and patted no backs that I could see. And he retired to his limousine as quickly as he could.

Hawaii's present governor, John Waihee, doesn't appear to suffer from shyness. But like Burns and Ariyoshi before him, he plays a private brand of politics, far from the glare of television lights and without the help of press agents. And, like his two immediate predecessors, he values consensus over confrontation.

In any other state in the union, the reserve shown by Burns, Ariyoshi and Waihee would constitute a serious political handicap. So too would their shunning of the press and their constant striving to forge a consensus. But Hawaii's voters deem these traits virtues. The Japanese, Korean and Chinese among them were brought up with a Confucian ethic of reserve. The aloha spirit and *ohana* (family feeling) of native Hawaiians are but another way of affirming consensus over confrontation.

At least one Hawaii politician, Sen. Daniel K. Inouye, has proven that the Islands' political style works well on the national political stage. During his almost 30-year long career in Washington, Inouye has seldom made headlines. Indeed, I once heard him boast that in his entire political career he had held only one press conference.

Yet Inouye is as popular in the nation's capital as he is in Hawaii. In 1973 his Senate colleagues chose him to serve on the Senate select committee to investigate Richard Nixon's role in the Watergate scandal. In 1987 they picked him to chair the Senate committee investigating the Reagan administration's sale of arms to Iran. And many Washington observers feel that Inouye might be the next majority leader of the United States Senate.

Why does Inouye inspire such trust among his senatorial peers? I'm convinced his ethnically derived sense of loyalty has much to do with it. Inouye's first-generation Japanese-American parents taught him the concept of *on*, reciprocal loyalty to those who have helped him. In the senatorial world of vote-swapping, Inouye's fellow senators know that his word is good. If they help him on a piece of legislation, they know that he will return the favor.

For the past quarter century, Hawaii's elected leaders have concerned themselves with a half-dozen principal issues: improving the life of Hawaii's laboring men and women through progressive labor legislation, extending equal political opportunity to all of Hawaii's people, building a first-class educational system, and protecting the Islands' environment and beauty. And a renaissance in Hawaiian culture over the past decade has resulted in increasing pressure on Island politicians to right some of the wrongs perpetrated on Hawaii's native people.

But perhaps no issue causes Hawaii's politicians and planners more anguish than the state of the Islands' economy. The Hawaii economy has been and remains narrowly based. In the early 19th century the economic health was dependent on sandalwood, from 1830 to mid-century it was dependent on the whaling trade, and from the mid-19th century to the mid-20th century, on sugar and pineapple cultivation. Since the end of World War II, the economic mainstays have been sugar and pineapple, the military, construction and tourism.

An economy so narrowly based can easily wither and die. Hawaii's sandalwood trade ended when the last sandalwood tree was cut and shipped to China – a mere two decades after the trade began. The discovery of oil in Pennsylvania in 1859 brought Hawaii's commerce in whales and their oil to a stop by the late 1860s. Hawaii's sugar and pineapple industry is in grave danger because both can be grown much more cheaply in parts of the world where labor costs are much lower than in Hawaii.

Likewise, today an airline strike could halt the flow of tourists to the Islands and cripple the state's economy. Or a strategic decision in the offices of the Pentagon could eliminate hundreds or thousands of jobs vital to Hawaii's economic well-being.

Tourism increasingly dominates the Islands' economy. Since statehood and the initiation of scheduled jet air service to Hawaii in 1959, the visitor industry has boomed. In 1986, Hawaii's beaches and warm temperatures lured 5,6 million visitors to the Islands. Over two-thirds of them came from the United States mainland, but Japan provided 19 percent, Canada 5.7 percent and Europe 1.2 percent.

Hawaii's visitors left more than $ 6 billion in the state in 1986, more than 30 percent of the gross state product of $ 16 billion. Their purchases continued the expansion of Hawaii as a service economy. While tourists sun themselves on Island beaches, Hawaii workers change their linen, prepare their meals, service their rental cars and sell them suntan oil.

Hawaii's geographical position gives it strategic military importance and, thus, its second largest industry. More than 100,000 soldiers, sailors, airmen and marines and their dependents are stationed in the Islands. In 1985 their salaries and the maintenance of Schofield Army Barracks, the naval shipyard at Pearl Harbor, Hickam Air Force base, the Kaneohe Marine Corps Air Station and Barbers Point Naval Air Station,

among others, brought 2.6 billion federal government dollars to Hawaii.

The defense sector directly employs 20,000 civilians in high-skill, high-paid jobs. It also provides employment to uncounted automobile salesmen, frycooks and entertainers who find their markets primarily among military personnel.

Construction is Hawaii's third largest industry. It accounts for a little less than 10 percent of Hawaii's gross state product, approximately $ 1.5 billion in 1985. Government contracts alone made up one-third of the total. Hawaii's burgeoning population, both visitor and resident, provide the demand for new hotels, more housing, better roads, and expanded health and recreational facilities. New construction activity seems to be everywhere.

Long the backbone of Hawaii's economy, the growing and processing of sugar and pineapple have been in rapid decline over the past decade. Indeed, in recent years Hawaii corporations have been closing marginal sugar plantations at an alarming rate. But sugar and pineapple still account for $ 563.3 million in sales, helping to make agriculture Hawaii's fourth largest income producer.

Sales of cut flowers, nursery products, papayas, macadamia nuts, vegetables and coffee have provided the growth in Hawaii's agriculture. Flowers and papaya have always produced profits for Island growers, but coffee is an example of a near extinct Hawaii product that has been revived. The development of the world gourmet coffee market has spurred Hawaii agriculturalists to cultivate long fallow coffee lands.

Despite the concern expressed by Island leaders about the narrowness of the state's economic base, Hawaii's economy has thus far proven singularly resilient. A quarter century ago Hawaii's agriculture dwarfed tourism as a contributor to gross state product. But as sugar and pineapple rapidly waned, tourism grew exponentially, employing those left jobless by closing plantations – and many more.

Indeed, despite strikes and national recessions, Hawaii's unemployment rate has remained below the national average. To be sure, a low unemployment rate alone does not mean a healthy economy. Critics of Hawaii's economy point out that maids, bellhops and rental car agents may be employed, but their jobs are low in both pay and status.

Hawaii's economic bases, however, have their advantages. Fields of green sugar cane and well-manicured rows of pineapples are beautiful, and beauty, after all, is one of the products Hawaii sells to its millions of visitors. Hawaii may not have a large manufacturing base – $ 1.7 billion in 1985 – but neither does it know industrial smokestacks belching pollutants into the Island skies.

And the absence of pollutants gives Hawaii hope for diversifying its economy further. Over the past two decades, Hawaii has gained international recognition as an astronomical laboratory. On the peak of Mauna Kea on the Island of Hawaii sit observatories operated by institutions from Hawaii, the Mainland and from around the world.

Hawaii's environmental offerings – from deep ocean basins to high volcanic peaks – promise other economic rewards. Since the oil shortages of the early 1970s, Hawaii has become a center for research on energy alternatives to fossil fuels. Hawaii's year-round tradewinds power fields of windmills both on the north shore of Oahu and in the Kohala district of the Big Island of Hawaii. Atop approximately one-fifth of all Hawaii homes sit solar panels to heat household water. On most of the state's major islands, bagasse, the residue from the production of sugar, is burned to provide power to Hawaii's major supplier of electricity. Perhaps most promising in the long term are the experiments being conducted on ocean thermal energy conversion. By harnessing temperature differences between deep ocean and surface waters, Island researchers hope to develop a limitless source of energy – the world's vast oceans.

However unpredictable Hawaii's economic future may be, I find the Islands not only a good place to visit, but a marvelous place to live. Hawaii's air is clean, its people warm and gracious and its beauty unparalleled. But I am most enamored by Hawaii's multi-ethnic politics. They are good for me, my wife and my family. The presence of a Hawaiian in the governor's seat, a Filipino in the lt. governor's chair, three Japanese-Americans and a Hawaiian in the United States Congress, and an ethnic melange in the state Legislature makes an important statement to all of us that we have opportunities, that we will be heard.

My wife is Filipino, my son half-Filipino, half-Caucasian, my adopted daughter one-quarter Japanese, one-quarter Korean and one-half Caucasian. When they watch Lt. Gov. Ben Cayetano being interviewed on the evening newscast or Daniel Inouye chairing an important Senate committee, my children will be reminded of the openness of Hawaii's society and of the opportunities available to them.

Hawaii's multi-ethnic politics affords them an opportunity unfamiliar to many minorities around the world: a license to dream limitless dreams. That's good for them and for all of Hawaii's children. It's an experience that, in a better world, all children could enjoy.

Notes on the Authors

Dan Boylan grew up in Indiana and Michigan. He first saw Hawaii as a United States Peace Corps volunteer trainee in 1966. Boylan returned to Hawaii in 1970 for graduate study, receiving his doctorate from the University of Hawaii in 1974. He is currently a professor of history at West Oahu College and a contributing editor to *Honolulu Magazine*. Boylan has written extensively on Hawaii's modern political history for *Honolulu* and other publications.

———

Carolyn A. Corn was raised in Panama and went to the United States for college. She earned a B.S. in botany at Oregon State in 1962, an M.A. in botany at the University of California at Berkeley in 1967 and a Ph.D. in the same discipline at the University of Hawaii in 1979. Corn has traveled extensively throughout Central and North America and has written numerous scientific articles. She has lived in Hawaii for more than 20 years and is currently working as a government botanist in Honolulu.

———

Carol Hogan grew up in Southern California and attended junior college there, continuing her education with courses at the University of Hawaii. She has been a free-lance photojournalist specializing in ocean recreation and outdoor sports for 20 years. Hogan contributes a weekly »Ocean Sports Journal« to *The Honolulu Advertiser* and writes for dozens of national and international publications. She is editor of Hawaii's only monthly ocean recreation publication, *Boating and Ocean Sports Magazine*. Hogan and her family built their first sailboat and left California in 1966 for an extended cruise through Mexico, Central America and the South Pacific. Experienced sailors, swimmers, bodyboard riders, cyclists and runners, Hogan and her husband rode their bicycles across the entire United States in 1981 and completed the 1982 and 1983 Ironman Triathlons.

———

Edward Joesting was educated in California and came to Hawaii in 1951. Having been a past president of the Hawaiian Historical Society, he has served as a lecturer at the University of Hawaii for many years. In 1969 he was presented an Award of Merit by the American Association for State and Local History. Joesting was author of two books about Hawaii with photographer Ansel Adams, as well as author and co-author of several other books of renown about the history of Hawaii. He passed away in Honolulu in 1986.

Bob Krauss grew up in the Midwest and received his degree in journalism from the University of Minnesota after serving in the U.S. Navy during World War II throughout the Pacific. He came to the Islands as a reporter in 1951, became a columnist in 1953 and has covered the Hawaiian chain, the South Pacific and Asia as well as Europe for *The Honolulu Advertiser*. His assignments have included the war in Vietnam, tidal waves, archaeological expeditions and canoe voyages. One of Hawaii's most versatile writers, Krauss has published nine books and many magazine articles.

———

Will Kyselka, brought up in Michigan, is a geologist by training. For the past 20 years he has been a professor at the University of Hawaii, Curriculum Research and Development Group, and a lecturer at the Bishop Museum Planetarium in Honolulu. He is author of three books on the geology of Hawaii and on astronomy. Kyselka is also producer and host of the radio program, »Science Hawaii.«

In a five-year-long collaboration, Kyselka and Nainoa Thompson have been involved in research in human navigation. Using the planetarium, they searched for clues in the sky for finding islands in the sea. Through their work there is now a much greater understanding of how Polynesians of old might have used the stars in finding their way over vast ocean distances to remote island destinations – without navigational instruments. Thompson and the crew of the double-hulled voyaging canoe, *Hokule'a*, have sailed 25,000 miles over the past decade to further understand the ancient art of wayfinding.

———

Andrew W. Lind was born and raised in Seattle, Washington, obtaining his B.A. and M.A. degrees in sociology at the University of Washington, and his Ph.D. in that discipline at the University of Chicago in 1931. He came to the University of Hawaii in 1927 as a research assistant in the sociology department and has continued to serve in that department, advancing to professor and department chairman and to director of the Social Research Laboratory. From 1947 to 1951 he was also dean of the Graduate Division. He retired in December 1967 as Senior Professor Emeritus of Sociology.

He received Fulbright grants for studies at universities in Jamaica, Bangkok and in Papua New Guinea. In addition to numerous articles and monographs his publications include five books. In 1986 a fund was established in his name to assure the continuation of the journal, *Social Process in Hawaii,* published annually, which Lind had initiated in 1935. Lind and his wife continue living in Honolulu, still actively sharing a life-long human and professional experience with students and faculty members.

Donald D. Kilolani Mitchell was brought up in Kansas and came to Hawaii in 1928. He earned his M.A. in 1936 at the University of Hawaii, and his doctorate at the University of California at Berkeley. He is a consultant in Hawaiian culture at The Kamehameha Schools in Honolulu. The Schools were founded for the education of Hawaiian youth a century ago and they are the sole beneficiary of the Bernice P. Bishop Estate which derives its income from the lands bequeathed to her people by Bernice P. Bishop, the last princess of the Kamehameha dynasty. Mitchell also works as honorary research assistant in anthropology at the Bishop Museum. He has served these institutions for more than half a century and is the recipient of awards and honors from a number of Hawaiian societies. He is also author of several books and articles about Hawaii and the Hawaiian culture.

Brian Nicol is editor and co-publisher of *Honolulu,* Hawaii's leading monthly magazine. He is a native of Minneapolis, Minnesota, where he attended the University of Minnesota, earning two bachelor's degrees and a master's. He was drafted into the U.S. Army in 1969 and first experienced Hawaii in 1970 while on R & R from Vietnam. Four years later he and his wife, Colleen, packed their bags and moved from Minneapolis to the Islands. He taught for a few years at Hawaii School for Girls, while his wife worked as a waitress at the Ilikai Hotel. He gradually phased out of teaching and into writing, eventually becoming editor of *Honolulu.* He and Colleen and their two boys live in Kaimuki, a quiet neighborhood behind Diamond Head.

Alan C. Ziegler spent his boyhood in the southeastern United States and has since traveled extensively on the Mainland and abroad. He attended the University of Tennessee and later the University of California at Berkeley, obtaining his B.A. and Ph.D. degrees in zoology and anthropology at the latter institution. From 1967 to 1983 Ziegler served as head of the Division of Vertebrate Zoology at the Bishop Museum in Honolulu and now works as an independent zoological consultant, being particularly involved with archaeological faunal analysis. He has also taught at various educational institutions in Hawaii, including Visiting Professorships at the University of Hawaii, and is the author of numerous scientific articles and book chapters.

Greg Vaughn, our principal photographer, was born and raised in California. He is a freelance photographer, and has lived and worked on the Big Island of Hawaii for more than half his life. His work has appeared in many magazines and books, such as National Geographic, Time-Life, GEO, Life, Travel & Leisure, National Wildlife, Aloha Magazine, Honolulu Magazine and others, as well as in corporate publications and broschures. He has been official photographer for the Ironman Triathlon and for the election campaigns of the last two governors of Hawaii.

Space does not permit writing about the many other photographers who have contributed their time and their art to this book.

Picture Contents